Report on Stained Glass Windows to Dr. James Thompson, Pastor

When I entered the church I put out of my mind everything I knew, heard or surmised. I approached the interior with only the thought I had, you had, the architects had, what we dreamed and hoped would be created.

The total concept I found breathtaking. Without doubt, I feel pleased the glass has accomplished its main purpose, to create a liturgical atmosphere to the greater glory of God.

As Henry Adams says in Mont Saint Michael and Chartres, the first command of the Queen of Heaven is for light and second and equally important, is color. Yes, we have color but the light and open effect has been maintained.

The color selection is exciting without being garish. The leaded stained glass truly sings and sings joyously. As to the iconography, we wanted the window to communicate the wonderful message of our faith but subtlety.

A stained glass window is the handmaiden of architecture. It must be treated as a part of the wall surface. It must be kept two dimensional, flat and decorative.

A window is to be an aid to the worship, not an idol or be worshipped. Like the Bible itself, a window has been read and re-read and then different and unexpected truths and incidents are discovered as the worshipper comes back time and time again. Start reading the Gospel of St. John. It moves you and stirs you but it takes many readings and much study to reveal the whole message. The same is true of a window.

I personally feel we have created stained glass that is both glorious in the best experience of the cardinal principle of our medium and a completely fresh and original concept.

The architects have given you an outstanding church and it has been so wonderful for one to have been able to create windows as they should have been designed and executed. This has not only been a wonderful experience and opportunity but the result is the greatest triumph. It has all been possible because of the working together and understanding with you and the architect.

Henry Lee Willet

Willet Stained Glass Studios, inc.

September 1980

Stained Glass Reflections

Shedding Light on the Windows of the First United
Methodist Church, Gainesville, Georgia.

Compiled by John McHugh

Table of Contents

Dedication

This book is dedicated in memory of Reverend Jim Thompson whose vision in large part is responsible for the beautiful stained glass windows of our church. Reverend Thompson was responsible for the subject matter of the windows and nurtured every step of their design and construction to ensure they represented appropriately the important stories of the Old and New Testament. The First Methodist Church of Gainesville was truly blessed to have at its helm Reverend Thompson during the move from the historic location in downtown Gainesville to the current location. His untiring desire for the new windows to be perfect and the old windows preserved, made the transition from the old to the new seamless and ushered in an optimistic future for our church.

Reverend Jim Thompson called our group of MYF seventh graders and us, as their counselors, over to a recently-poured section of shiny grey concrete. It was a Sunday afternoon, and we had come to visit the site of our new church on Thompson Bridge Road. Sweeping his large hands to help us visualize what was taking shape as the sanctuary, he told us, "This is where the pulpit will be, and over there will be the altar railing. On these two sides, there will be wooden arches with beautiful stained glass windows with images depicting stories from the Bible." I will never forget the next moment. Jim grasped our hands and had the group form a circle. Then in that wonderfully deep resonant voice he began to sing, "It only takes a spark to get a fire going." We all joined him in the rest of that favorite song we had sung with him on retreats and on camping trips with the youth, "and soon all those around can warm up to its glowing."

A few months later, in the summer of 1980, we made the move from Green Street to Thompson Bridge Road. It was a Sunday morning full of emotion – sadness because we knew we were worshipping for the last time as a congregation in a building full of memories and tradition – and also excitement because we were moving to a new structure with the potential for greater growth and ministries. After the service, we followed Jim Thompson, church leaders, and acolytes as they carried the altar Bible, paraments, and candles out the front doors and down the steps.

The stained glass windows were removed from the sanctuary of the old church. It was sometimes easy to forget they were crated and stored behind concrete block walls in the red clay soil, underground at the new church for many years – during a time period that included various leaders, and expansions, and capital campaigns. Finally, when the time was right, several of the windows were carefully installed in the fellowship hall and the library. Then the rest were placed in the chapel. When we first saw the old windows again, in their new setting, it reminded me of seeing the features of grandparents in their grandchildren.

Those old windows had fascinated me as a child. I had stared at the beauty of sunlight streaming through them when I first joined the church. Later when I was a high school student, Jim Thompson became our minister, and I continued to enjoy the windows as I listened to his sermons and to the poignant, original stories he wrote for Christmas Eve. They were part of the sacred setting when Jim performed our wedding ceremony at the old church. After thirteen years as our minister – overseeing the site selection, the construction, and the furnishing of the new church, Jim Thompson continued his ministry as District Superintendent of the Griffin District. Later he was assigned as Minister at Decatur FUMC and upon retirement returned to our church as a faithful member, singing in the choir and often teaching classes. He established a ministry in Honduras, leading volunteers in building a clinic, a school, and a church among other projects.

In June of 2012, when we celebrated Jim Thompson's life at his memorial service, we did so in the sanctuary he had worked so hard to make a place of worship and beauty.

He was the spark that made it possible for so many to continue to feel the glow of God's love.

Marsha Hopkins

This is the window of The Good Shepherd referenced in Dr. Thompson's Sanctuary story. It is located in The First United Methodist Church Chapel and was moved from the Green Street Church.

Sanctuary

Stories from the Heart

The Christmas Eve crowd was beginning to disperse now and the continuous bumper to bumper traffic circling around the Gainesville square was thinning. The sun had traveled so majestically through a crisp, pristine December day and was now glowing red in the West, casting long shadows across the confederate soldier standing guard in lonely, silent vigil toward the north. Above the now diminishing cacophony of traffic and shopping floated the crystal clear note s of the Salvation Army bell, held in the tired, numb fingers of a young volunteer left guarding the kettle during the last closing hours of the season.

On the corner, a young man stood leaning casually against the front of the drug store. He was tall and lean, but thick of chest and shoulder. His ragged jeans fit loosely around his waist and thighs and his faded blue t-shirt was mostly hidden by an oversized brown corduroy coat. His sharp, dark brown eyes darted back and forth watching the passers-by. As he watched and waited for the precise moment that he needed, his mind traveled over the events of the last few months and over the experiences that had brought him back to North Georgia and to this particular point in time. For Luke, it had been one bad choice after another. From the moment he dropped out of school in Rabun County to the time when he ran away from home and began hitch-hiking to Atlanta and then New Orleans and Dallas and finally The Golden Gate City of San Francisco, he had tried it all; pot, cocaine, heroin, and alcohol. He knew what it was like to wake up in a stupor, covered by his own vomit, on the bare floor of an abandoned house in the urban renewal district and to ramble through garbage cans behind city cafes and restaurants looking for some morsel of food on which to exist for one more day. He had stolen, shop-lifted, purse-snatched, sold his body, and worked in demeaning jobs. He would do anything to stay alive. Through some miracle he had managed not to become addicted to anything but pot. He didn't know why. It was probably because he never really had enough money to buy the hard stuff.

All of that had come to an end a month ago. The loneliness, the emptiness, the meaninglessness of his existence finally began to haunt him and he had set out again by thumb to Georgia and home. Now here he was in Gainesville, still without food or a place to go. For three nights he had slept in an empty old Victorian house down on Broad Street, entering after dark, when no one would see him. His situation was desperate. He had nothing.

Suddenly, the lull in the crowd he had been waiting for took place. With his heart pounding in his temples, he strode to the Salvation Army booth. Pushing aside the speechless young man, he grabbed the kettle and fled down Bradford Street and up another toward Green. He could hear shouting and footsteps behind him on the square. Spying a large red-brick building, he ran up the steps, tugged open the door and fled down a dark hall. For a long time, he waited breathlessly in a side room trying to stop the pounding of his heart and the shaking of his hands. Finally, when it seemed certain that no one had followed him, he crept out of the room, up the stairs, and into a large room which was lighted by the glow from the tallest, most beautiful Christmas tree he had ever seen. With a start, he realized that he had hidden in a church, of all places! He almost smiled at the irony of it all! Quickly he made his way to into one of the pews and hiding the kettle under a pew, he stretched out full length to wait until it was completely dark.

By now the last few rays of the sun were dancing on the jewel-like colors of the stained –glass windows. From where he lay, Luke could see one of the windows clearly. It was a picture of Jesus carrying a lamb and suddenly he remembered.

He remembered the little white frame church on a high red clay bank above the Tallulah River. He remembered the times before his father died when he and his family would go to that little church at Christmas time. He remembered the candles in the clear glass window shedding their light out on the green, frost covered rhododendrons surrounding the little church. He remembered the big pine wreath on the weathered front door and the preacher reading the scripture from the old walnut pulpit. Most of all he remembered the music. He remembered his Aunt Kate playing the autoharp and his dad's deep baritone voice singing the harmony to "O Come, all Ye Faithful." After the services, they would go home, popcorn on the log fire and drink cider until the kids were shooed to bed to wait for Santa Claus.

5

How many years ago that seemed to Luke, even though he was still only seventeen. How from that beginning had he ever ended up like this? How had it all changed, or was he the only one who had changed?

For Luke, life started to go downhill when his father died. Something happened then. Everyday became dull and monotonous and existence seemed too much of a struggle. There was not much joy or laughter anymore, not even from mama. She had to work too hard and the strain of holding the family together was taking its toll. She didn't mean to be unpleasant or to nag, but she did and gradually Luke decided he couldn't take it any longer. That was when he quit school and ran away.

Suddenly Luke was aware of a door opening. Someone had come into the room and without realizing what he was doing, Luke sat up. "Hello," the man said. "How are you? Have you come for the Christmas Eve service? It will be starting in about forty-five minutes."

"No," Luke answered. "I just came in to rest a minute and get warm. I've been shopping downtown."

"Good! We're glad to have you. Have you been here long?"

"Only a few minutes," Luke answered. "I've been looking at the windows. I especially like that one."

"Yes, that's one of my favorites, too," the man said. "Jesus the Good Shepherd. I always imagine how glad the lamb must have been to be found by the shepherd and taken back home."

Luke was silent for a long time then quietly he spoke, "Sir, could I talk with you for a moment?"

"Certainly," the main said, sitting down on the pew in front of him.

"You know I used to go to the church at Christmas time." There was a long pause and he continued, "But I haven't been for several years now."

"I understand," the man smiled. "That happens to so many of us. We don't even realize it, but gradually, like the sheep, we nibble here and there without watching where we are going until one day we lift our heads and discover we're a long way from the shepherd and home."

No one spoke for a few minutes. Then Luke said quietly, "Can a man really start over, Sir?"

The man, sensing the awesome sacredness of the moment, whispered, "Yes, that's what Christmas is all about. Changing direction and going home."

Luke sat quietly, gazing up at the stained glass. "Sir, would you see that the Salvation Army gets this?" Luke said as he pulled the kettle from under the pew and handed it to the man.

He slid from the pew and started up the aisle toward the door. Stopping for a moment he turned and said quietly, "Thank you sir. I won't forget this night."

When Luke stepped out the door of the church, fresh, crisp air bathed his face. From the church tower, the Christmas bells were playing a carol. Somehow the words meant more to Luke that night than they had ever meant before.

"Born to raise the sons of Earth,

Born to give them second birth."

In his heart he knew he would find someone that very night who would give him a ride across the mountain. He was going home!

Dr. James Thompson

7

Window Gazing

Beauty, majesty and mystery define the stained glass windows of Gainesville First United Methodist Church. As we enter the sanctuary, our eyes are immediately drawn to them. The room itself is an architectural wonder to behold, but our mind's eye is quickly captured by the colors, contours and grandeur of these windows, as the chronicle of the ever-abiding story of God's redemptive purposes for God's people.

A simple glance will not suffice. No, these windows demand a through gazing; a focused intentionality; a surrender to that which is masterful.

For those of us blessed with the gift of sight we take for granted the ability to look through a window. We do it countless times each day. We check the weather by looking outside. We tell our grandchildren to not get up until the light is coming through the window. We find ourselves window shopping looking at the newest styles. We look out to see the beauty of God's creation. We even look through the windows of our home and are hit with the fact that they need to be cleaned! But when we step inside the sanctuary of this church we know those windows are different – these windows have a way of looking at us! (Perhaps they are noticing that we might well need a cleansing of our own, and we have come to the right place to receive it.)

One of the distinguishing characteristics of stained glass windows is the need for light. The light not only brings out the unique colors but also allows the various figures to take definite shape. However, an observer of these windows finds another aspect of their beauty. Extra beauty comes in the way the light hits the glass. From the bursting forth of a new day until the sun sets in the west the windows become a continual story. Different light brings its own unique distinction. The light makes all the difference. Take the time to gaze at these windows at different times and in different seasons. You will be amazed at the beauty and grandeur.

We, as Christians, know the difference the light makes in our lives. That light is Jesus. Gaze into his eyes and discover new life. It is the life Dr. Thompson preached and we are fortunate that he left these windows as a part of his legacy.

Keep gazing.

Dr. Phil DeMore

THE OLD TESTAMENT SIDE

PATRIARCHS   PROPHETS   KINGS

The Hand of God

Genesis 1:26

"I will make man to be like me. Man and woman will be the leaders over the fish, the birds, and over all animals created to fill their needs-like chickens, cows, and sheep, and man will be over all the Earth. All the creatures that move along the ground are put there for man and woman."

The hand of God reaching down to create earth is depicted here. The image of the near-touching hands of God and Adam in Michelangelo's fresco Sistine Chapel ceiling painted circa 1511–1512 has become one of the single most iconic images of humanity.

The Hand of God

This was written for children. License has been taken in the interpretation of Genesis 1:26. The intention is to help them know and remember, as they see the stained glass to be aware of the continued Love, Generosity, and Power of our Heavenly father.

Billie Thompson

The little four-year-old girl with curly, blond hair and sparkling blue eyes stood on the wooden bridge that crossed the creek on the family farm. As she tossed a stone in the slowly moving water, she made a discovery.

"Daddy, when I threw the rock into the creek, it made circles in the water. "

The circles got bigger and bigger as she decided to demonstrate this wonder.

"Why does it do that?"

As spring began, yellow, white and lavender crocus poke their sleepy heads through the scattered snow in the front yard.

"Oh-h-h, Daddy! Look at this pretty white flower. It smells so good! Did Mamma spay it with her perfume? What do we call it? What do we call it?"

Her father told her the flower was called a gardenia.

"Will it bloom all summer?" she asked.

"Why does it smell so good?"

The little four-year-old was named Joy, and she was full of questions, as most four-year-olds tend to be.

"Oh, Daddy, look at that little bird. He has a pretty colored place under his neck!"

"Oh, yes, Joy!" said Dad.

"We call him a hummingbird. He flies very fast. Look at his wings move. He likes to sip the juice from summer flowers, just as you like sipping through a straw!"

"Where does he live, Daddy? How did he get there?"

"Why do animals that live in our yard like each other so much? I've seen lots of things like birds, squirrels, turtles, and butterflies in our yard. I know they like each other 'cause they don't try to scare or hurt each other."

"Joy, you know how we like to talk about how God, Our Father in Heaven, made everything? Our Bible tells us that God made the Earth, the sky, night and day, the mountains, and the seas. He made all the birds, animals, bugs, flowers and trees. After God made all these things, He made man and woman. God called the man Adam and he named the woman Eve. When God made man and woman, He said they should be the leaders over all He had made. He gave everything He had made to man and woman. He still gives everything to us today.

How can we show God we love Him, too? Let's smile more, say thank you more, be kind to people even when they may not be nice to us. Let's not say ugly things about other people. We wouldn't want others to say bad things about us, would we?

Let's tell each other when we see some special gift God has made for us! We will remind each other that all these beautiful sunsets, fall leaves, seashells, and waterfalls came from the hands of God."

Let's learn a Bible verse:

Deuteronomy 6:5 "Love the Lord you God with all your heart."

Let's bow our heads and pray.

Thank you, God, for all the beautiful and loving things you have made for us. Help us take good care of the gifts you give us. Amen.

Isaiah 45: 12

It is I who made the earth and created mankind on it. My own hands stretched out the heavens; I marshaled their starry hosts.

Abraham and Isaac-God Will Provide

Genesis 22:11-14

And Abraham lifted up his eyes, and looked, and behold behind him a ram caught in a thicket by his horns: and Abraham went and took the ram, and offered him up for a burnt offering in the stead of his son.

The phrase, "A ram in the bush" is often used as an expression to describe something that God has provided one in a time in need. This particular figure in our stained glass is one of the hardest icons to discern as a ram in a thicket on the Old Testament Side.

Genesis 22: 1–3, 9–14 (NRSV)

1 After these things God tested Abraham. He said to him, "Abraham!" And he said, "Here I am." 2 He said, "Take your son, your only son Isaac, whom you love, and go to the land of Moriah, and offer him there as a burnt offering on one of the mountains that I shall show you." 3 So Abraham rose early in the morning, saddled his donkey, and took two of his young men with him, and his son Isaac; he cut the wood for the burnt offering, and set out and went to the place in the distance that God had shown him.

9 When they came to the place that God had shown him, Abraham built an altar there and laid the wood in order. He bound his son Isaac, and laid him on the altar, on top of the wood. 10 Then Abraham reached out his hand and took the knife to kill his son. 11 But the angel of the Lord called to him from heaven, and said, "Abraham, Abraham!" And he said, "Here I am." 12 He said, "Do not lay your hand on the boy or do anything to him; for now I know that you fear God, since you have not withheld your son, your only son, from me." 13 And Abraham looked up and saw a ram, caught in a thicket by its horns. Abraham went and took the ram and offered it up as a burnt offering instead of his son. 14 So Abraham called that place "The Lord will provide"; as it is said to this day, "On the mount of the Lord it shall be provided."

It's the ultimate test: taking something you love, something you've prayed for, and maybe even dreamt about all your life, and then giving it away. How do you do it? It's so painful. The idea is almost unthinkable. But then you remember, "Grace." God has given us life, sustained it, and even forgiven it in the many moments when we never deserved it. You begin to remember, "All I am and all I have are gifts from God; I am a life created out of Divine Love and Grace." And so in this moment we can be encouraged that the One who is asking the impossible **from** us did the impossible **for** us.

There is no sacrifice we can make that escapes God's understanding or ability to be in solidarity with us. In Jesus Christ we have "God with us," identifying with every struggle, every need, and every seeming impossibility, but "…nothing will be impossible with God" (Luke 1:37). Abraham learned this first hand as he walked up that mountain. You know the tension was mounting. Every step he took he was one step closer to losing his son. In his mind, there was nothing easy about obeying God. He had already left his home, his family, and probably took on some ridicule for following after a voice that was leading him to a land that had yet to be disclosed. Nothing made sense. Or did it?

See, we have the upper hand. Because of Abraham's faithfulness and the revelation of Jesus Christ, we understand that anything asked or expected of us comes from a place of Divine love. God asks that we be obedient children. Why? Because He is a loving Father who seeks our good. There is nothing to dispute such a claim because both the Biblical witness and the testimony of the Church through the ages is that God loves us and seeks to make us whole.

So, did Abraham really sacrifice his son? The narrative says no and yet Abraham continued not only up the mountain but drew the knife. The Lord had to stop him from carrying out his command. My point is that in Abraham's mind, he had resolved to carry out the wishes of God. He put God first and in doing so God put Abraham's heart at ease. It goes to show that God was with Abraham. The Lord just wanted to see that Abraham was with God. Abraham discovered for himself where his faith was and if he could love the Lord in such a devoted way. It was here that he loved the Lord all the more because he now knew that "The Lord will provide." Abraham sacrificed the thing he loved most for God in his heart and in the end kept his son, too. It's called a win-win and only at the deepest levels will we experience such victories.

I hope you'll see the ram in the bush in our beautiful stained glass windows and remember for yourself that "The Lord will provide." But what I ultimately want you to remember is that the ram caught in the bush is a sign that all things in your life are motivated by Divine love. God cares for you and is leading you to salvation. This is proven through Jesus' sacrifice, as He willingly laid down His life for us. As He said, "I came that they may have life, and have it abundantly" (John 10:10b).

Rev. Whit R. Martin
Pastor, New Liberty United Methodist Church

Moses and the Ten Commandments

Exodus 24:12

The LORD said to Moses, "Come up to me on the mountain and stay here, and I will give you the tablets of stone with the law and commandments I have written for their instruction."

Exodus 32:15-16, 19.

There were two sets of stone tablets. Moses threw down and smashed the first set when he returned from the mountain and found the Jews worshiping a calf.

Study Guide for Moses Window

Moses was one of the great men of the Old Testament and of human history. God through him caused Pharaoh to free the Hebrew slaves. He led them through the wilderness for forty years until they were ready to enter the Promised Land. Through Moses God gave us the Ten Commandments which for Jews and Christians are the foundation of morality, and also they are the foundation of the U.S.A. legal system. People are still benefiting from what Moses did.

In this paper Moses' life is the theme. His life will be broken down in sections as described in the book of Exodus.

Ex. 1:6-12

The Hebrews entered Egypt and became slaves. Each section of Moses' life will have scripture references of key verses. Read them carefully. The Holy Spirit can speak to you through scripture.

Ex. 2:1-1-0

Moses Was Born into Slavery and Trained in Pharaoh's House

Though Moses was born in slavery, he was raised in Pharaoh's house because he was adopted by Pharaoh's daughter after he was found floating in the Nile River. He received an excellent education. He never let having been born into slavery deter or hinder him. Every person is called to give himself or herself to God and seek His mission for his or her life. We are all given a box of tools (talents). Each person is called to be the person God wants us to be. Moses did not allow his slavery origin deter him or use this as an excuse in answering God's call.

Understand that Moses received the best education or training of his time. This was part of his preparation for his mission in life. This tells us the importance of getting our education early. Do not wait until mid-life to wake up to its importance. The apostle Paul was well educated and trained when Jesus called him. Moses was prepared before he was called.

Ex. 2: 11-15

Moses saw an Egyptian beating a Hebrew. He killed the Egyptian; therefore he had to flee to Midian from Egypt. Long years there caused him to realize the consequences of his sin. *A person can control his or her choices, but cannot control the consequences.* "The wages of sin is death." This act by Moses, we believe, helped him to see the consequences of his wrong (immorality). Think of Judas who betrayed Jesus, Peter who denied that he knew Jesus, and Paul who held the coats while Stephen was stoned. Their choices had serious consequences. We either keep the moral law or it will destroy us. The answer for Christians is in the forgiving, redeeming love of Jesus Christ. Moses's life showed him the consequences of his sin.

Moses did wrong and he paid the price. This true of everyone. The Egyptians did wrong when they made slaves of the Hebrews and think of the price they paid. When slaves were brought to America wrong was done. Think of the harm that has been caused to all persons involved. We believe that Moses, because of his killing the Egyptian was helped to realize the importance of the Ten Commandments.

Ex. 3: 1-12, 4: 10-12

Moses Was Called to Lead the Hebrews Out of Slavery to the Promised Land

Suggested Songs – "I Will Sing a Song of the Saints of God"

No. 712, United Methodist Hymnal

"Go Down, Moses"

No. 448, United Methodist Hymnal

Moses was a *shepherd*, but God wanted him to be a *deliverer*. David was also a *shepherd*, but God wanted him to be a *king*. As you think about God's call to Moses; meditate on what God wants you to be and do then trust Him to cause to happen.

God got Moses' attention through the bush that burned, but not consumed. When he heard God's call to bring the Hebrews out of Egypt he objected and asked, "Who am I that I should? They will not believe me." God told him, "I will be with thee." Ex. 3:12. Th4:10. Then Moses raised a second objection. "I am not eloquent." Ex. 4:10. God told him, "He (Aaron) shall be thy spokesman...unto thy people." Ex. 4:16. Moses finally agreed to go. What a decision and a commitment! Then his father in law, Jethro said, "Go in peace." Ex. 4:18.

When God calls we need to listen and do what He wants us to do. Our lives will not be fulfilled until we do His will. When someone else is called of God we like Jethro need to give them our support and encouragement.

Ex. 11:1-10, 12: 1-13, 12: 29-40, 13: 17-22, 14: 1-12, 14: 21-31

Moses Led the Hebrews Out of Slavery

Moses went to Egypt and demanded that Pharaoh free the Hebrew slaves so they could return to their homeland. After many plagues Pharaoh still refused. The last plague God told Moses will cause Pharaoh to free the slaves. Moses said, "Thus saith the Lord, All the first born shall die..." including people and beasts. Ex. 11:5. The Hebrews as Moses instructed put the blood of a lamb on their door post to spare the first born Hebrew children. On the given night it happened as God said. In the confusion as the first born of Egyptians and beasts died the Hebrews (600,000) left led by Moses and Aaron. This experience is the basis of the Jewish Passover observance. At the Red Sea with the Egyptians in pursuit, the waters parted for Moses and he led his people through on dry land. When the Egyptians followed the wind stopped and the army drowned. This was one of the great miracles of history. Moses and his people began forty years of wandering in the wilderness.

It is worth noting God provided direction and miracles as needed. When you say yes to God He does not give a blueprint to follow. We live by faith and He opens the doors as needed.

This whole experience of deliverance is one the best examples in human history of "from slavery to freedom." Think about Abraham Lincoln's role in freeing the slaves in our history and Martin Luther King's role in the Civil Rights Movement. Both were shot. It is a miracle Moses survived. What a man of faith!

Ex. 20: 3, 4, 7, 8, 12-17

Moses Receives the Ten Commandments from God

Suggested Song- "I Am Bound for the Promised Land"

No. 724, United Methodist Hymnal (Sing chorus several times.)

The Ten Commandments were the major preparation for the Hebrews entering the Promised Land. This was also Moses' main contribution to mankind. As the Hebrews wandered for forty years in the wilderness Moses sought to get them strong enough to possess the Promised Land. This was done by training them to live by the Ten Commandments. This task was not easy. Read them carefully.

These guides, I repeat, are the basis of Jewish and Christian morals and the foundation of our legal system in our country today. If we break them and do not repent and change, they will break us. We are free to make choices, but we cannot control the consequences of these choices. Moses words are as up to date as when he first received them from God. His life continues to be an inspiration to all who think about what God did through him. Everyone needs to keep asking the question, "What does God want me to do for Him and others?"

Closing Thoughts

When we were in Rome, Italy and saw the sculpture Michelangelo had made of Moses we looked in awe at the work of art he had carved. He had put in stone the greatness of this man of God, a champion of human freedom and morality. May Moses' life continue to inspire us to be the person God wants us to be. If we will *listen* He will tell us our mission. If we will *trust* God He will cause our mission to become a reality.

Rev. Thomas H. Johnson, Sr. and Emmie Carlton Johnson

When Moses was chosen by God to lead the Jews out of Egypt he was unsure of himself because he stuttered.

Exodus 4: 10

And Moses said unto the LORD, O my Lord, I am not eloquent, neither heretofore, nor since thou hast spoken unto thy servant: but I am slow of speech, and of a slow tongue.

Exodus 4: 14-15

And the anger of the LORD was kindled against Moses, and he said, Is not Aaron the Levite thy brother? I know that he can speak well. And also, behold, he cometh forth to meet thee: and when he seeth thee, he will be glad in his heart.

And thou shalt speak unto him, and put words in his mouth: and I will be with thy mouth, and with his mouth, and will teach you what ye shall do.

Although Moses led the Jews out of Egypt God did not allow him to cross the Jordon River or see the Promise land he had worked so hard to reach

Numbers 20: 8, 11-12

Take the rod, and gather thou the assembly together, thou, and Aaron thy brother, and speak ye unto the rock before their eyes; and it shall give forth his water.

And Moses lifted up his hand, and with his rod he smote the rock twice: and the water came out abundantly, and the congregation drank, and their beasts also.

And the LORD spake unto Moses and Aaron, Because ye believed me not, to sanctify me in the eyes of the children of Israel, therefore ye shall not bring this congregation into the land which I have given them.

August 9, 1982

Reverend Jim Thompson to Henry Willet

"On the positive side, I like the symbols very much – especially the changes you have made. I must confess that I even like Moses, though I realize you couldn't completely part with his horns."

Exodus 34:29-32

*When Moses came down from Mount Sinai with the two tablets of the covenant law in his hands, he was not aware that his face was **radiant** because he had spoken with the LORD. When Aaron and all the Israelites saw Moses, his face was radiant, and they were afraid to come near him. But Moses called to them; so Aaron and all the leaders of the community came back to him, and he spoke to them. Afterward all the Israelites came near him, and he gave them all the commands the LORD had given him on Mount Sinai.*

Notice that Moses in our stained glass windows has horns. Many scholars feel that Moses depicted with horns is the result of a mistranslation of Moses returning from the mountain with his face being described as "radiant." Over time some scholars have mistakenly translated radiant as "having horns."

21

The Passover

Exodus 12: 12-13

On that same night I will pass through Egypt and strike down every firstborn of both people and animals, and I will bring judgment on all the gods of Egypt. I am the Lord. The blood will be a sign for you on the houses where you are, and when I see the blood, I will pass over you. No destructive plague will touch you when I strike Egypt.

The Jewish celebration of The Passover is intertwined with the Christian observation of Easter. This is because Jesus was crucified and resurrected shortly after the Passover Last Supper.

Easter falls on a different Sunday each year is because of the way that day is determined. Easter is the first Sunday after the first full moon after the spring equinox. This method always assures that Easter (The Resurrection) occurs after the Jewish celebration of Passover just as it did in The Bible.

Exodus 12: 22-24

"You shall take a bunch of hyssop and dip it in the blood which is in the basin, and apply some of the blood that is in the basin to the lintel and the two doorposts; and none of you shall go outside the door of his house until morning. "For the LORD will pass through to smite the Egyptians; and when He sees the blood on the lintel and on the two doorposts, the LORD will pass over the door and will not allow the destroyer to come in to your houses to smite you. "And you shall observe this event as an ordinance for you and your children forever."

The Hyssop Plant-A herbaceous plant native to the Middle East and used as an aromatic herb and medicinal plant. In the Passover passage it was used as a paint brush to apply the blood.

Lintel- A lintel is defined as a structural horizontal block that spans the space or opening between two vertical supports.

PASSOVER

Exodus 12:1-13

When Israel went out from Egypt,

the house of Jacob from a

people of strange language,

Judah became God's sanctuary,

Israel God's dominion.

The sea looked and fled;

Jordan turned back.

The mountains skipped like rams,

the hills like lambs.

Why is it, O sea, that you flee?

O Jordan, that you turn back?

O mountains, that you skip like rams?

O hills, like lambs?

Tremble, O earth, at the presence

of the Lord, at the presence of the God of Jacob,

who turns the rock into a pool of water,

the flint into a spring of water.

Psalm 114, NRSV[1]

---

[1] Scripture quotations are from the NRSV unless otherwise noted.

Getting ready to be Set Free

It is night in the land of Egypt. Darkness has descended over every field, every street, and every house. Gathered in their homes, the Hebrew slaves begin to eat, their voices hushed. The tension surrounding them is palpable. This meal will be their last in the land of Egypt. Never again will they eat, looking over their shoulders in fear; never again experience the cruelty of their oppressors. They are preparing to take their first steps as free women and men: steps that will lead them out of bondage, and toward the land of their ancestors.

Their story began with the great-grandson of Abraham and Sarah. Jealous of their younger brother, Joseph, Jacob's older sons sold him to slave traders. The saga of Joseph and the Hebrew sojourn in Egypt is recorded in the latter part of the book of Genesis. (Gen 31-50) The total length of time this family and their descendants spent in Egypt is recorded as being 430 years. (Ex 12:40) Their fateful progression from residency to forced labor is introduced with the words, "Now a new king arose over Egypt, who did not know Joseph." (Ex 1:8) The reference is, most likely, to Seti I. (1308-1290 B.C.) After so long a time, the Israelites had become a large segment of the population, and were now viewed as a security risk. Thus the oppression began.

Pressed into hard labor, the Hebrew slaves were forced to build cities. Yet even as their lot became more and more desperate, they continued to thrive and increase in number. It is at this point that the command to kill all of the Hebrew baby boys is given. Baby Moses is rescued from this fate by the strength, the wit, and the love of three women: his mother, Jochebed; his sister, Miriam; and the daughter of the King of Egypt. (Ex 1-2) The death of the reigning king is reported, but any glimmer of hope that conditions might improve is dashed when a new king, probably Ramases II, (1290-1224 B.C.) ascends the throne, and becomes even more oppressive.

This chapter of the story closes with words that become the hinge upon which the door to deliverance will open: "The Israelites groaned under their slavery, and cried out...and their cry for help rose up to God." (Ex 2:23-26) Thus, a long and arduous battle with the king of Egypt begins. The words of the familiar African- American spiritual capture its essence:

> When Israel was in Egypt's land,
> let my people go;
> Oppressed so hard they could not stand;
> let my people go.
> Go down, Moses, way down in Egypt's land;
> Tell old Pharoah to let my people go!

On the eve of their departure they have gathered, under the cover of darkness. Explicit instructions have been given for this final meal. A lamb, either from the sheep or the goats, was to be obtained, one for each family or group of families; a year old male, without blemish. On the fourteenth day of the month, the lambs were to be slaughtered at twilight and roasted over the fire. All of the meat was to be eaten that night, along with bitter herbs, representing their slavery, and bread made without leaven. (Ex 12:3-10)

The meal was to be eaten hurriedly, in preparation for their departure:

Eat it with your cloak tucked into your belt, so you can get up in a hurry and be on your way.

Eat it with your sandals on, an exception to the usual rule of removing them, so you are ready to walk out of the house.

Eat it with your walking stick in your hand. You're going to need it on the journey.

Don't even use yeast in the bread. There's no time for it to rise. (Ex 12:11)

This was not to be a leisurely dinner, with time for conversation and visiting. God is about to open the door to the house of bondage. If you become too comfortable where you are; if you fail to carry out these instructions, you won't be ready, and you might be left behind.

At the heart of the preparations is the instruction to smear blood from the slaughtered lambs above and on either side of the doors of their homes. Then come these chilling words: "I will pass through the land of Egypt that night, and I will strike down every firstborn...both human beings and animals...The blood shall be a sign for you...when I see the blood, I will pass over you." (Ex 12:12-13)

We now arrive at the most significant element of this feast: the name by which it is to be called. It is the passover of the Lord. Later, as it becomes a ritualized observance, it becomes Passover, with a capital "P." At this point, it is descriptive of God's favor to God's people: I will pass over your homes, when I see the blood on your doors.

Even for those of us who know this story well; for those of us who believe we know the God of this story, it is difficult not to cringe at the pronouncement of death upon the Egyptians, including that of many innocents. There has been a prolonged and intense struggle with a cruel and oppressive ruler, during which time this king has had numerous opportunities to comply with God's demand for justice. History has repeatedly shown that ruthless people who come into power do not give it up without a fight, and sometimes it is a fight to the death. Still, it is bothersome. In the language of modern day war, it would be called collateral damage, which is very bothersome.

One thing we can say with certainty about the God revealed in the scriptures: God always fights on the side of the oppressed. Woe to those who fight in opposition. It is important to keep that in mind as we read the pronouncement upon the Egyptians. The intent is not to harm the Egyptian people, nor to destroy Egypt. God's action is centered around one objective: to free the Hebrew slaves. Yahweh's vengeance toward the Egyptians is that of a mother bear whose cubs are being threatened. She will go to any lengths to protect them.

The whole point of this saga is just that:

God has seen their misery.

God has heard their cry.

God knows their sufferings.

God will deliver them.

God will bring them out of Egypt.

God will bring them into a good land. (Ex 3:7-8)

That God heard, and heeded the cry of these oppressed people; that God acted on their behalf, has become a message of hope for oppressed people everywhere.

The Passover and the giving of the Torah are the touchstone events in the history of the Israelite people. Both confirm, and set in stone, as it were, the covenant God made with them. The artist's representation of each can be located in the pane left to the center on the Old Testament side of the windows, placed diagonally to each other. The icon picturing the Passover depicts two things: The framework of a Hebrew house, with blood streaming down the door, and an angelic being hovering over, passing over it. A careful reading of this account will note that an angel is not mentioned as the death-dealing agent in this attack. It is clear that this is very personal to God. The existence of *God's* firstborn is being threatened. This will be God's doing: "*I* will pass through the land…" (Ex 12:12)

It is not, however, out of keeping with Old Testament theology that an angel is seen as a personification of God. In fact, "the angel of the Lord (Yahweh)" stands out from that of angels in general. The angel of the Lord is not a heavenly being subordinate to God, but the Lord in earthly manifestation. (Gen 16:7-13; Ex 3:2ff) The artist's rendering of the passing over of the Hebrew homes would be in keeping with this understanding. It could also fall in line with the recalling of this event in Psalm 78: "God let loose on them his fierce anger, wrath, indignation and distress, a company of destroying angels." (Ps 78:49) "Thus God led his people out like sheep, and guided them through the wilderness like a flock." (Ps 78:52)

And so it is, that at the midnight hour, when hope is fading and nothing seems possible, God performs the act that will cause the door to swing open into freedom. It will be remembered as such a significant event, that it will change the way time is measured: "This month is to be the first month of the year for you." (Ex 12:2) No longer are they to use the calendar of the Egyptians, a symbol of their slavery. From now on, they are to have their own calendar, and the first month of the year will always be the anniversary of their deliverance from bondage. The passover feast will be, not only a remembrance, but a symbol and a sign of a fresh start. When, in future generations, their children will ask about its meaning, their answer shall be: "It is the passover sacrifice to the Lord, for he passed over the houses of the Israelites in Egypt, when he struck down the Egyptians but spared our houses." (Ex 12:27)

They are poised and ready to go. God's forceful words, through Moses, to the Pharoah, "Let my people go," are now paralleled by the unspoken, yet equally powerful question to the people:

Are you ready to be set free?

Rev. Patricia M. Southerland

The Last Supper

Luke 22:14-22

When the hour came, Jesus and his apostles reclined at the table. And he said to them, "I have eagerly desired to eat this Passover with you before I suffer. For I tell you, I will not eat it again until it finds fulfillment in the kingdom of God." After taking the cup, he gave thanks and said, "Take this and divide it among you. For I tell you I will not drink again of the fruit of the vine until the kingdom of God comes." And he took bread, gave thanks and broke it, and gave it to them, saying, "This is my body given for you; do this in remembrance of me." In the same way, after the supper he took the cup, saying, "This cup is the new covenant in my blood, which is poured out for you."

The above figure is a depiction of The Last Supper. Dr. Thompson had to ask that the stained glass representing the wine be changed to purple and to be made more prominent.

Do you see which figure represents Judas in the stained glass? Hint: He is the one without a halo.

THE LAST SUPPER

Mark 14:12-26

Once again, it is night; this time, in the city of Jerusalem. Darkness has settled over every hill, every street, and every house. With the coming of dusk, the descendants of those who came out of Egypt during the exodus are gathered around the table to partake of the Passover meal. As they had for centuries, they recounted the story of the night in which God delivered them from bondage. Much has taken place in the history of the Israelites. They have experienced other seasons of hardship, and at times have been driven from their land and taken into slavery. Yet God has never forsaken the covenant made with them: I will be your God; you will be my people. (Ex 6:7) Nor have they been left without hope. Messages of assurance have been spoken through the mouths of prophets, along with the promise of a new deliverer.

The city was flooded with pilgrims. Jerusalem was considered the only proper place to observe Passover. Added to the 80,000 already living in Jerusalem, another 100,000 poured into the city. During times of Jewish dispersion, the cry of those for whom this trip was not possible has been, "Next year in Jerusalem!" It was a time during which expectations were high. Living under Roman occupation, each year at Passover, hope would rise: Will this be the year in which God will deliver us again? On other occasions, uprisings had taken place, and dreams had been dashed with the disappointment promised by a would-be deliverer. At such times, retaliation by the Romans was swift and brutal.

Early in all of the gospels, we find Jesus coming into conflict with the religious authorities of the day. This tension escalates, until finally, the decision to have him killed is made. (Jn 11:53) Having sought a way to arrest Jesus, the chief priests and scribes determine that Passover week is not a good time. The risk is too great. If a riot were to break out among the people, the consequences would be terrible. It is into this dangerous, volatile atmosphere that Jesus enters Jerusalem a few days before Passover. His disciples have tried to discourage him from coming, but he is determined to eat the Passover meal with them. He does not enter quietly, but with prophetic symbolism: riding on a donkey, amid the waving of Israel's victory symbol, the palm branch. (Jn 12:12-15) Shouts of "Hosanna!" mirror later cries of "Crucify him!

On the day of the Passover, Jesus sends two of his disciples to make the preparations. According to Luke, the two were Peter and John. (Lk 22:8) They were to look for a man, carrying a jar of water, a secret sign intended to hide the place of the meal from Jesus' enemies. A man carrying a water jar would have been easy to spot. Women normally carried the water. They were to follow the man to the pre-arranged place, where the owner would show them to the guestroom: a large, upstairs room, furnished and ready. (Mk 14:13-15)

The largest room in a house would have been the room upstairs, because it only had to support the ceiling. That it was a furnished room meant that it had a reclining table with mattresses placed around it. Originally the rule for eating the Passover meal was standing, reminiscent of the Hebrew slaves' haste in leaving Egypt. When the Romans gained control in 63 B.C., only free people could eat reclining. Slaves had to stand. The rule for eating the Passover meal changed: on this one night of the year, you must eat it reclining, even if your family is among the poorest, to show that you are free, and that God has brought you out of Egypt.

The more wealthy families would have had a large U-shaped table, with an entrance on one side for serving. The Passover meal was to be eaten reclining on the mattresses around the table, leaning on the left elbow, leaving the right hand free for eating, with one's feet behind, away from the table. At every dinner party, there was an order to the seating. Jesus advised his disciples about this at an earlier time: When you are invited to a dinner at someone's home, don't go in and take a place of honor. Take a lower seat, and if the host wishes, you may be invited to move to a more important place. (Lk 14:7-11) At a U-shaped table of this type, the person of most prominence, usually the host, would sit at the left hand wing of the table as you look into the "U." On either side of this person would be an assistant, one to the right and one to the left. (Remember the argument among the disciples about who would be the greatest, and the request by the mother of James and John that they be seated on Jesus' right and left?) (Mt 20:20-28)

On Passover evening, we find Jesus and his twelve disciples, gathered in such a room, reclining around the table. Jesus would have taken the place of host, in the middle of the left wing of the table, flanked on either side by persons of his choosing. The idea of the person on the right was taken from a military motif: sword on the right, shield on the left; the one who would guard and protect. Seated to the right would have been the most trusted person. The gospel of John identifies the person to Jesus' right as "the one whom Jesus loved." (Jn 13:23) The person on the left would have been the chosen guest of honor.

The icon in which the last supper is pictured is located at the bottom of the central panel of windows depicting events in the New Testament, as if everything above has its foundation in this Passover meal. Rising from it, side by side, are the cross and the phoenix, drawing the eye upward, toward the ascension of Jesus. In this artist's rendering of the scene, the disciples are gathered around a table, with Jesus at far right, lifting the cup. In contrast, Judas, who will later betray Jesus, is seated at the opposite end of the table. His head is bowed, indicating shame, and perhaps, Jesus' pronouncement of woe upon him. (Mk 14:21)

In each of the gospels, Judas is mentioned for the first time in the listing of Jesus' disciples, and in the context of his betrayal of Jesus. (Mk 3:19; Mt 10:4; Lk 6:16; Jn 6:71) He is always named last. There has been much speculation concerning Judas' motive for betraying Jesus. Some have attempted to put Judas in a more favorable light by suggesting that he was hoping to force Jesus' hand; expecting that Jesus would call upon all of his resources to overthrow the Roman occupation. While a more attractive idea than others, nothing is found in any of the gospels, or elsewhere, to suggest this.

Mark offers no explanation as to Judas' motive. He simply states that Judas went to the temple authorities, the chief priests and scribes, with the proposal to betray Jesus, and that they offered him money. (Mk 14:10) In Matthew, Judas asks the question of them: "What will you give me if I betray him to you?" implying that his motive was greed. (Mt 26:14-15) At that point he is given thirty pieces of silver.

In John's narration, Judas is named as the one who protests the pouring of costly ointment over Jesus' feet, seemingly indignant over the wasting of something that could have benefitted the poor. The writer of John is quick to explain that Judas didn't care about the poor, but that he was a thief, and as the keeper of the disciples' treasury, he stole from it. (Jn 12:1-8)

Each of the gospels describes an anointing of Jesus' feet by a woman. Only John places the event in the home of Mary, Martha, and Lazarus, and names Mary as the one who poured her precious ointment over Jesus' feet. In Matthew, Mark, and Luke, the woman performing this beautiful act of service is unmanned, but Jesus says of her actions, "wherever the good news is proclaimed in the whole world, what she has done will be told in remembrance of her." (Mk 14:9) Her devotion toward Jesus is in sharp contrast to Judas' betrayal of him. Both will be remembered for their actions during Jesus' last hours.

It is difficult to imagine how one could perform the horrific act of betraying a close and trusted friend, simply to acquire material gain. Yet greed is a powerful force. We see it around us and participate in it ourselves on a daily basis. Greed (avarice) is listed among the Seven Deadly Sins. Like a spider web, the more deeply one becomes drawn into it, the more difficult it is to extricate oneself. Bit by bit, one is plunged into darkness, betraying everything that is good, and truthful, and of God. Perhaps Jesus' description of Judas as "a devil" is one way of speaking of Judas' descent down that dreadful path, being drawn more toward evil than to God. (Jn 6:70-71)

Luke comments that, prior to his visit to the chief priests, Satan entered into Judas. (Lk 22:3) The word *Satan* means "adversary;" one who is working against, in this case, against God. On another occasion, Jesus addressed Peter as Satan: "Get behind me, Satan! You are setting your mind not on divine things but on human things." (Mk 8:31-33)

Words from the hymn, "God of Grace and God of Glory," seem to describe what happened to Judas: "Shame our wanton, selfish gladness, rich in things and poor in soul." Judas sought to become rich in things, to the exclusion of everything else, leaving him in the terrible, vulnerable position of being poor in soul. Judas' story could be any of our stories. Failing to align himself with Jesus meant making a deal, not only with the chief priests and scribes, but with the forces of evil. To paraphrase the conclusion of the hymn stanza: Judas missed the Kingdom's goal. And so it is, that on that fateful night, Judas' misguided act provided the adversaries of Jesus with the opportunity they had been seeking.

One cannot help but wonder what would have happened to Judas if he had returned to the community in repentance, seeking reconciliation with Jesus' followers instead of ending his own life in despair. Might one of the gospels have included a post-resurrection encounter between Jesus and Judas, as there was with Simon Peter? (Jn 21) Could Jesus' words from the cross, "Father, forgive them; for they do not know what they are doing," (Lk 23:34) extend even to Judas?

These are questions that remain unanswered, insofar as the gospel writers are concerned. Following Judas' betrayal of Jesus, he is not mentioned again, except in Matthew, who reports Judas' repentance and his returning of the pieces of silver to the temple leaders. Overcome with remorse, Judas hangs himself. (Mt 27:3-5) Matthew's casting of Judas is harsh, holding him up as a model of failed discipleship. But for Matthew, the point is not merely the tragic situation of Judas. More important to his telling of the story is the conflict of kingdoms, and how terrible it is to cast one's lot with the wrong side.

Another question that comes to mind has to do with the relationship between the will of God and Judas' participation in Jesus' death. In each of the gospels, it is clear that Jesus' last journey to Jerusalem, and subsequently to the cross, was of divine origin. Was Judas just a pawn, used to accomplish God's purposes? If so, how can he be held accountable? The gospel writers do not answer this question, but neither do they try to parcel out responsibility for Jesus' death between God and humanity. God is fully sovereign; humanity is fully responsible. That Jesus *gave* his life; that it was not taken from him, stands at the heart of Christian theology. Yet Judas made the decision to play a part in Jesus' arrest and crucifixion, and subsequently had to bear the burden of his actions.

Perhaps the most telling observation that can be made concerning Judas derives from Jesus' posture toward him during the Passover meal. All four gospels report the announcement of Jesus during the meal that one among them would betray him, followed by the disciples' shock and questioning of who it might be. The NIV translation of John 13:22 reads: "His disciples stared at one another, at a loss to know which of them he meant." Peter gestures to John, who is seated next to Jesus, to ask him who it is. Jesus answers John's inquiry with the words, "the one to whom I give this piece of bread when I have dipped it in the dish." (Jn 13:23-26) The one to whom Jesus offers food as a gesture of friendship, is the one Jesus knows to be the betrayer.

Although the text provides no specific information as to Judas' position at the table, Jesus' reference to dipping the bread in the bowl and giving it to him might indicate that Judas was seated next to Jesus; on his left, in the place of honor. That was the way one designated the guest of honor: by taking some bread, dipping it in the bowl, and putting it into the mouth of the person to the left. If this reconstruction is correct, it would be a striking example of loving one's enemies. Normally, a traitor in the midst would be exposed and expelled from further contact with the group. At the very least, Jesus includes Judas in table fellowship, offers him hospitality, and conceals his identity from all except the beloved disciple.

One final note concerning the artist's rendering of Judas: His bowed head is not adorned by a halo, in contrast to the other disciples. While appreciating the visual reminder of Judas' treacherous role, one has to question the validity of the halos surrounding the heads of the others, considering their behavior that night! While Simon Peter's outright denial of Jesus is remembered most often, Mark records, sadly, that following Jesus' arrest, they *all* deserted him and fled. (Mk 14:50) As Jesus was crucified, only the women who loved him remained, watching from a distance. (Mk 15:40-41; Mt 27:55-56; Lk 23:27, 49, 55-56) John pictures Mary, the mother of Jesus, his mother's sister, Mary the wife of Clopas, and Mary Magdalene near the cross, as well as the beloved disciple. (Jn 19:25)

So, who gets halos and who doesn't? At the core of Christian theology is the belief that the underserved grace of God is the only means by which one has merit; that any halos we might suppose we or others deserve, are not to be placed over our heads because of our own striving. As far as our musings about the fate of Judas, we shall leave that to God's discretion, as is the case for all of us.

As Jesus shared the Passover meal with his disciples that night, they recalled God's gracious and redemptive acts of the past: God's overcoming the armies of Egypt, and their escape into freedom. Together, they remembered the message of the prophets: the promise that one day God's reign would be complete, and God's people would live in peace. When Jesus lifted the bread and broke it; raised the cup to offer it, this long-term perspective hung as a backdrop.

But this night of remembrance was different. It was to be their last together. Jesus knew it, and yet, on that night, he was able to preside at the table; to assume the role host; to offer the ancient words of blessing over the bread; to lift the cup and give thanks to God.

It is worth noting that, on the eve of his death, Jesus gave thanks to God. Knowing at that very hour, the plot to destroy him was unfolding, Jesus gave thanks to God. Knowing that one of his own disciples was about to betray him, Jesus gave thanks to God. Knowing that his closest friends would soon desert him, Jesus gave thanks to God. Knowing that before sundown of the next day, his own body would be hung on a cross; his blood spilled upon the ground, Jesus gave thanks to God.

We are reminded of it every time we observe Communion: "On the night in which he gave himself up for us, Jesus took bread, blessed it and broke it... and when the supper was over, he took the cup, and gave thanks to God..."

Mark concludes his telling of this Passover with the words, "When they had sung the hymn, they went out to the Mount of Olives." (Mk 14:26) When I was a child, I thought that hymn was, "Blest be the Tie that Binds," the hymn sung following Communion in the church my family attended. While not a bad choice, I don't think Jesus and his disciples knew that hymn.

The hymns to be sung at Passover were Psalms 113-118, called the "Hallel (Hallelujah) Psalms." Psalm 113-114 are sung at the beginning of the meal; psalm 115-118, at the end. Psalm 114, in particular, is a hymn of praise for God's deliverance from Egypt. Portions of Psalm 118, the last of these psalms, are frequently quoted by the New Testament writers: vv22-23 being understood as referring to the Messiah; the speaker in vv5-18, 28 identified by the early Christian community as Jesus.

For all the gospel writers, Psalm 118 provides a means of understanding and expressing the significance of Jesus. His life, death, and resurrection thus become extensions of God's saving activity in the exodus, and later, in the return from exile. This Psalm has been given a prominent place in the worship life of the church, highlighting Jesus' entry into Jerusalem on Palm/Passion Sunday, and also during the celebration of the resurrection on Easter, above all "the day on which the Lord has acted." (Ps 118:24 NEB) These are the hymns Jesus and his disciples would have sung before leaving for the Mount of Olives: Hallelujah! Praise the Lord!

When we recall the events of that night, we most often remember Jesus' prayer of anguish in the garden: "Abba, Father, for you all things are possible; remove this cup from me."(Mk 14:36) But looking back, we see that Jesus also gave thanks. The steadfast assurance in the faithfulness of God that permeated Jesus' life enabled him to lift his voice, not only in anguish, but also in thanksgiving and praise; culminating in this extraordinary expression of trust: "Yet, not what I want, but what you want." (Mk 14:36)

As he offered the bread and the cup to his disciples that night, Jesus reinterpreted its meaning: "This is my body which is given for you. This cup that is poured out for you is the new covenant in my blood. Do this in remembrance of me." (Lk 22:19-20) The Greek word translated *remembrance* is *anamnesis*. Its meaning is somewhat different from the English word *remember*. It is not entirely possible to capture its meaning in English. It can also be translated *recalling*. Do this for my recalling. Do this and you will be recalling me.

One way we use the word *recall* means the same thing as to remember: Do you recall that person's name? Another use of recall is more immediate. When you are recalled for jury duty, they are not just remembering you, they are expecting you to show up! When Jesus told his disciples to observe this meal in remembrance of him, he did not mean that they were to sit around and reminisce about the good old days. The gift Jesus gave for remembering is, by the presence of the Spirit, that of being able to recall him to us; not a vague memory from the past, but a living presence.

The affirmation of Christ's church proclaims our faith in the covenant relationship set forth that night. The prayer before coming to the table is called, "The Great Thanksgiving." It speaks of God's redemptive acts of the past and points us toward the promises of the future, culminating with our corporate witness:

Christ has died.
Christ is risen.
Christ will come again.

Each time we gather around the table, we are reminded of God's faithfulness, and of the relationship we have with each other. We are relatives: blood relatives, you might say. This table draws us together as family. It also offers us an opportunity to have a different frame of reference for our lives. Paul writes to the church at Corinth, "Our Paschal lamb, Christ, has been sacrificed. Therefore, let us celebrate the festival, not with the old yeast, the yeast of malice and evil, but with the unleavened bread of sincerity and truth." (1Cor 5:7-8)

No longer are we required to live according to the old calendar, defined by slavery to negative, destructive patterns of thinking and acting. We are given a new beginning and a fresh start. John Wesley believed that the bread and cup that we receive become vehicles through which the grace of God flows. He called it, "a means of grace."

God still comes at the midnight hour, when hope is fading and nothing seems possible, and opens the door that leads to deliverance. Interpreted in light of the new covenant, are these words:

O let us all from bondage flee,
let my people go;
and let us all in Christ be free,
let my people go!

Sharing the bread and the cup together, we are invited to contemplate the question posed to the Hebrew slaves:

Are you ready to be set free?

Rev. Patricia M. Southerland

35

Joshua and the Trumpet

Joshua 6: 20

So the people shouted when the priests blew with the trumpets: and it came to pass, when the people heard the sound of the trumpet, and the people shouted with a great shout, that the wall fell down flat, so that the people went up into the city, every man straight before him, and they took the city.

God often times uses people who at first glance seem ill suited to the task. In the story of Joshua and Jericho, Rahab a harlot (prostitute), is very instrumental in allowing the Jews to enter the city and aid in their victory.

Joshua 6: 17

And the city shall be accursed, even *it, and all that* are *therein, to the LORD: only Rahab the harlot shall live, she and all that* are *with her in the house,* because *she hid the messengers that we sent.*

JOSHUA FOUGHT THE BATTLE OF JERICHO

We face battles every day. We battle with others: our family, our friends, our co-workers. We battle with ourselves: our circumstances, our health, our emotions. We battle with nature: ice storms, tornados, our use of natural resources. Sometimes we even battle with God. We don't think He is handling things like we think He should. The Bible never promises that Christians won't face battles. In fact, it is the exact opposite. The Bible guarantees that we will face battles just because we are Christians.

So what is the difference on the battlefield for those who follow Christ and those who don't? The difference is in what we see in the midst of battle. Do we see giants or grasshoppers? Do we see other people or circumstances as giants – strong and powerful – and ourselves as insignificant grasshoppers – small and powerless?

In Numbers 13 God instructed Moses to send out twelve spies, one from each tribe, to explore the land of Canaan -- the Promised Land for the Israelites. After 40 days of exploring, ten spies saw obstacles but two spies saw opportunities. In their field of vision was the same thing, but it was their interpretation of what they saw that was different.

"Not so much what life brings to us in her hands as what we bring to life in our spirits makes the difference between people" noted Harry Emerson Fosdick in his book, The Secrets of Victorious Living. Our interpretation of a battle determines how we approach it. It is that "different spirit" found in the two spies, Caleb and Joshua, that influenced their interpretation of what they saw. When we see through the lens of God's power and God is in control then mountains can be moved and walls can come tumbling down.

The Battle of Jericho is an amazing story filled with turns and twists that confound the mind of man. It is a "God story" – a story that is so outrageous, so unlikely that the only way the Israelites could succeed was through the power of Almighty God. It is in Joshua 2 that we meet the prostitute Rahab, a person who the world saw as having no worth. Rahab not only becomes a hero in the Battle of Jericho, but she becomes part of the lineage of Jesus Christ. Something God alone could see. In Joshua 3 the mighty leader Joshua marches toward Jericho, not with swords and might leading the way, but following the priests and the Ark of the Covenant. Why? Because God is leading the way into battle. Without God's guidance the Israelites don't even know where they are going. The battle is God's. God assures Joshua that Jericho will fall and God gives Joshua his instructions. Joshua is obedient. While Joshua doesn't see how marching around Jericho and blowing trumpets will bring down walls, he does see and know a God who keeps his promises. Joshua know he has a choice: He can focus on the problem or he can focus on The Promise.

One day a father and his young son went out for a day of fishing. It was just the two of them in a small row boat on a large lake. Suddenly the father saw a storm fast approaching on the horizon. The father knew that they must quickly get the boat to shore or risk being caught in the storm. The father also knew that the sight of the fast approaching storm would scare his young son and that the child might panic and not be able to help row the boat back to shore. The father told his child, "I want you to keep your eyes on me, just me. Keeping looking at my face and let's row this boat back quickly back to shore." The child, trusting in his father and keeping his focus on his father's face stayed calm as the two rowed the boat back to the safety of the shore.

What do you see? Where is your focus in the midst of battle?

"Turn your eyes upon Jesus.

Look full in wonderful face.

And the things of earth will grow strangely dim

In the light of His glory and grace."   Hymn by Helen H. Lemmel, 1922

Joshua 3:5 reminds us to live with a sense of wonder; to be eager, alert and expectant to what God is doing around us. It is when we lose sight of a God who can do the incredible and the impossible, that fear and frustration take over. Know that God has greater things in store for the tomorrows of your life. God loves you. The hope of the world is the hands of those who believe and follow God Almighty, who can and will do the impossible.

"Be strong and courageous. Do not be terrified. Do not be discouraged. For the Lord your God is with you wherever you go." Joshua 1:9

Lee D. Highsmith

The Completed Temple

*The completed temple shown above is located at the very top of the
"Kings" lancet on the Old Testament side of the Sanctuary. The window to
the right of David represents the materials he collected to build the temple.
To the left of Solomon is the destroyed temple.*

The Temple. The idea for this house of worship was planned in the mind of
King David, "a man after God's own heart" (I Samuel 13:14) by the Spirit.
Certainly, David had already shown his wisdom in choosing Jerusalem as
his capital city. It was a pagan city and not claimed by any of the tribes of
Israel, therefore averting any jealousy between the tribes.

Certainly, David's desire was to build this great sanctuary for the Lord. In
an ironic twist, God forbade David from building the temple personally
because he was a king of war. (1 Chronicles 28:3) This reminds us of God's
sovereignty and how far above His thoughts and actions are than ours.
(Isaiah 55:8-9) It should be an encouragement to us all that God recognized
David's desire to build the temple. We are blessed not only for what we do

The Completed Temple and the Star of David

1 Chronicles 17:1

*After David was settled
in his palace, he said to
Nathan the prophet,
"Here I am, living in a
house of cedar, while
the ark of the covenant
of the LORD is under a
tent."*

1 Chronicles 22:19

*Now devote your heart
and soul to seeking the
LORD your God. Begin
to build the sanctuary of
the LORD God, so that
you may bring the ark
of the covenant of the
LORD and the sacred
articles belonging to
God into the temple
that will be built for the
Name of the LORD."*

for Him but also what we WANT to do for Him. David purchased the land (II Samuel 24:18-24), procured the materials (I Chronicles 22:2-16), and appointed his son, Solomon as its builder.

Exactly what the temple looked like is uncertain. We do know that King Solomon spared no expense it appears. It was 180 feet long, 90 feet wide and 50 feet high. The stone walls were lined with carved cedar which were covered with gold. In the holy place, there were several pieces of furniture; alter of incense, ten golden lampstands, and ten tables of showbread.

The most important room, the holy of holies, had only one piece of furniture but a very important one- the Ark of the Covenant. This is where the priest would enter once a year during Yom Kippur and offer a sacrifice for the people of Israel.

Even though Solomon's temple was destroyed, the importance of the temple concept remained. The rebuilding of the destroyed temple is recorded in the book of Ezra. It was destroyed only to be rebuilt by Herod beginning in 19 B.C. This is the temple that Jesus knew.

Herod's temple was more political than spiritual. In fact, two of the most fascination events took place in the temple involving the life and death of our Lord. Jesus became so angry in the way the temple was being abused that he overturned the money making ventures that were taking place there. And at the time of His death, the temple veil was torn from top to bottom, illustrating God's availability to all of us who are His.

The history, its structure, its New Testament significance are all important. But what does the temple mean to us and how can it apply to us?

It is wonderful to know WE are the temple of the living God! (Cor. 6:16) The picture of Solomon's temple with its outer court, inner court, and the holy of holies is a prototype of us physically, mentally, emotionally, and spiritually. We are "fearfully and wonderfully made", just like the physically amazing temple, we have "the mind of Christ" as represented by all the pieces of "worship" furniture in the inner court, and we have our own holy of holies, where we've been made alive by Jesus sacrifice.

The temple was a picture, a snapshot of where God's presence resided. Did that temple confine God- certainly not. We are His temple. And just like the temple of old, that was cared for and maintained with such integrity; so should we honor Him in the things we think, the things we do, and the places we go, because we are- the temple.

Rev. Tim Barrett

Solomon and Wisdom

1 Kings 6:11-13

Now the word of the Lord came to Solomon, "Concerning this house that you are building, if you will walk in my statutes and obey my rules and keep all my commandments and walk in them, then I will establish my word with you, which I spoke to David your father. And I will dwell among the children of Israel and will not forsake my people Israel."

1 Kings 6:37-38

In the fourth year the foundation of the house of the LORD was laid, in the month of Ziv. And in the eleventh year, in the month of Bul, which is the eighth month, the house was finished in all its parts, and according to all its specifications. He was seven years in building it.

Solomon was also known for his wisdom and this figure shows the sword with the scales of justice. In 1 Kings 3:16-28 two women contest being the mother of a child. Solomon ruled, *"Cut the living child in two and give half to one and half to the other."* At this the real mother said that the other woman could have the child and this showed Solomon who the real mother was and he awarded the child to her demonstrating his wisdom to Israel.

Solomon – A Man of Greatness

Humanity has always admired people of greatness. Men and women who have accomplished the unimaginable, reached the pinnacle of power, or become the fashion of fame have captivated the spirits of mankind with a passion that is unmatched. World leaders, athletes, musicians, and actors or actresses seem to be the standard of our dreams. But what is greatness? How is greatness accomplished? Is it possible to lose greatness? Here is the story of one man of greatness that once had it all and then forfeited it.

Solomon, the Son of David, King of Israel, was a man of greatness who lived in the tenth century B.C. His greatness I will list in three categories: 1) Solomon was a man of great blessings 2) Solomon was a man of great responsibilities and 3) Solomon was a man of great failure.

A Man of Great Blessings

Some people may identify Solomon's blessings as being born to a king, living in a palace, and having the wealth of the world. But Solomon's blessings go beyond what we can see with the human eye.

Part of the Plan of God

In the Bible, in I Kings 1, we are told how Solomon becomes king. David, his father, is nearing death. King David promises to make Solomon king and has Solomon anointed. But becoming the king is not the blessing, being part of the plan of God is. God had promised David that he would give him a son who would reign after David and his kingdom would last forever. Solomon was not even born at the time of the promise but God was at work to fulfill his eternal plan for mankind. So the first blessing to Solomon was becoming king of Israel which was part of God's plan.

When we understand that God has a plan for all of humanity and that he is at work to fulfill that plan, it is a blessing to know that we are part of it. The promise that God made David, and Solomon became a part of that plan, was the plan of salvation for humanity. Through David and Solomon, God would bring the King of kings to this earth. His name is Jesus. As eternal King, Jesus is Savior of humanity. Wow! How blessed Solomon was to be of the plan of God.

God Answered Solomon's Prayer

The second blessing given to Solomon was when Solomon, as the young king, understood that he was not capable on his own to lead God's people. Solomon prayed to God and asked for wisdom to lead the nation. Solomon knew that the people of Israel were special to God and he did not want to lead them wrong. What a blessing it is to be able to meet with God in prayer and make request for God's help in our lives so that our lives will honor him. I Kings 3:10 states, "And the speech pleased the Lord, that Solomon had asked this thing." (KJV)

God not only answered Solomon's prayer for wisdom but also chose to give him wisdom far beyond that of his peers. God also gave Solomon what he did not ask for. God gave him wealth, honor, and **greatness**. Every blessing from God is great but God blessed Solomon greatly.

How greatly blessed all of humanity has been in God revealing Himself to us. God wants us to know Him, worship Him, and serve Him through the King, Jesus Christ.

A Man of Great Responsibilities

It is not hard to imagine the pressure that Solomon felt being King. Being King brought great responsibilities. Solomon was responsible to lead God's people Israel, build a temple for Israel to worship God at, and to follow God obediently. In I Kings 9:1-11, God explains to Solomon that obedience and faithfulness to God would bring about the fulfillment of God's promise to David. Talking about responsibility! The promise God made to Solomon's father now rested upon his leadership. Anyone who wants to honor their parents would not want to be the reason for not receiving the promise of God, but that was now the responsibility of Solomon.

The fact is we are all responsible for our own personal lives before God. But think just a moment about the responsibility that you have before God in connection with the lives of other people. We are responsible for our actions that affect other people. How our decisions affect those around us is something that our society does not give enough consideration to. It is a great responsibility to live for Jesus Christ in such a way as not to hinder others from experiencing the grace of God in Salvation.

A Man of Great Failure

For Solomon, he had a great start to life. Tragically it did not end in greatness. We see this all too often today. Men and women have great potential and the opportunity of God's plan and God's blessings to be fulfilled in their lives. Because of bad decisions and the rejection of God's word people turn from God and the promises of God for humanity are not fulfilled.

Solomon loved God, I Kings 3:3, but Solomon loved himself more. This is the first great failure in any person's life. The Bible goes on to say, "But King Solomon loved many strange women" and "clave unto these in love." (I Kings 11:1-3) Solomon's problem was that he wanted to please himself more than he wanted to please God. God warned Solomon about this before it ever happened (I Kings 11:10) but Solomon refused to follow God.

Solomon's great failure would be costly. The nation of Israel would be attacked by an enemy which meant that the peace they had enjoyed was gone. After Solomon's death the nation would be split into two kingdoms. How would you like to be remembered as the king who cost the nation its peace and unity? How would like to be remembered as the one who cost your family its peace and unity? There is no substitute for following God with our whole heart.

One of the last things said about Solomon was this, "and Solomon did evil in the sight of the LORD, and went not fully after the LORD, as did David his father." (I Kings 11:6) Greatness has various ways of application. Don't let your greatest "greatness" be described as "a great turn away from God."

Rev. Joey Pritchett

1 Chronicles 17:1-4, 10b-12

"Now when David settled in his house, David said to the prophet Nathan, 'I am living in a house of Cedar, but the ark of the covenant of the LORD is under a tent.' Nathan said to David, 'Do all that you have in mind, for God is with you.' But that same night the word of the LORD came to Nathan, saying: 'Go and tell my servant David: Thus says the LORD: You shall not build me a house to live in"…."Moreover I declare to you that the LORD will build you a house. When your days are fulfilled to go to be with your ancestors, I will raise up your offspring after you, one of your own sons, and I will establish his kingdom. He shall build a house for me, and I will establish his throne forever."

David and His Harp

1 Samuel 16: 23

And whenever the tormenting spirit from God troubled Saul, David would play the harp. Then Saul would feel better, and the tormenting spirit would go away.

In this Biblical narrative known by many as the Davidic Covenant, David prepares to enter a time of peace and rest as he settles into his house, he genuinely seeks to bring glory to God by building a temple to serve as a house for the ark of the covenant of the LORD. David's sincere desire is to see the God of the Israelites glorified and honored. However, God sends word to David through the prophet Nathan, that David was not to build the temple, one of his David's sons would build the temple. In God's response to David, He also tells David that He will build David a house, a dynasty of David's ancestors, which ultimately leads to Jesus.

David was set to build God's temple in Jerusalem as a true desire of his heart, but upon hearing God's response to his desires, David submits to God's will over his own and accepts God's will that ultimately Solomon would build the temple. Later in 1 Chronicles, the author tells us that David makes all the preparations for the temple to be built, including securing building materials, workers, support for the inexperience Solomon, funds for the project, and the plans for the temple delivered by God. All of these materials, funds, people, and plans are secured by David to ensure that God's will would be carried out by God's chosen builder: not David, but Solomon.

Among many lessons we can learn from David's role in the planning and construction of the temple, two stand out as lessons for the people called God's church. Many times, we desire to rush into an endeavor to bring glory to God and to expand God's Kingdom without submitting our plans to God for His blessing first. David had done so in the past, but had learned his lesson. This time, he was submitting his plans to God before continuing any further. This time, however, God's answer to David was no. He had plans for someone else to accomplish his works. How often do we take the time to submit our hearts desires to accomplish something for God to Him before we rush into the plans and works we desire? Are we truly willing to submit our plans and to hear the answer God gives? Are we willing to hear "No" or "Later"?

Rev. David Burchett

Jesus the Prophet

Mathew 21: 11

And the multitude said

this is Jesus the prophet

of Nazareth of Galilee.

JESUS AND THE PROPHETIC TRADITION

The center panel of the East window portrays Jesus as successor to the Judaic prophetic tradition. In Luke we learn that after Jesus' baptism and temptation in the wilderness, he visited his local synagogue and read aloud from the scroll of Isaiah:

> "The spirit of the Lord is upon me because he has anointed me; He has sent me to announce good news to the poor; to proclaim release for prisoners and recovery of sight to the blind; to let the broken victims go free, to proclaim the year of the Lord's favor." (Luke 4: 18 – 19)

Then, after remarking that the text had come true, his friends and neighbors became astonished and asked, " Is this not Joseph's son?" Whereupon, Jesus made the famous remark, "No prophet is honored in his own country." (Luke 4: 24-25). Sure enough, then and there, his neighbors turned against him and tried to throw him off a cliff. (Luke 4: 29-30)

Thus was the remainder of Jesus' life and ministry foreshadowed.

Biblical prophets address the failure of the people of Israel and Judah to honor the Covenant with God originating in the Exodus and manifest through the events of history. A recurrent theme is the practice of shallow religion and pagan worship, but an equally important theme is to call for justice for the poor and powerless. As advocates for the disadvantaged they speak against social injustice and especially those in power who promote it. Challenging the powers that be has never been popular with the home folks. Jesus must have been painfully aware that he was required to be a stranger in the midst of his own people. Prophets may comfort the oppressed, but they make those comfortably in power mighty uncomfortable.

Looking at the East window with the prophetic tradition in mind, additional symbolism is apparent. First, Christ is depicted at the apex plainly clothed, perhaps in sackcloth, in contrast to his portrayal on the West window in royal trappings. This reminds us of His humility and identification with the poor and powerless.

Second, below Jesus on the left appears a grasshopper associated with Amos(Amos 7:1), a famous advocate for the poor and helpless, and, on the right, Isaiah who first advanced the idea of a suffering servant to identify with the oppressed.(Isaiah 53).

Third, below the prophets is a rainbow, the sign of the Noahic covenant, arching through the panels depicting Amos' grasshoppers, Daniel's lions, and Jonah's whale, which suggests that the Noahic Covenant was between God and "all living things of every kind" (Gen. 9:16-17), as reaffirmed by John 3:16 : "For God so loved the world."

So how are we, the champions of capitalism and the consumer economy, likely to react to the prophets of today who decry the destruction of helpless species and advocate for the poor who stand to suffer the most from our desecration and plunder of this miraculous and beautiful planet created and loved by God?

I suspect we will not honor them for they make us uncomfortable indeed.

Frank Armstrong

The Locust

Amos 7:1-3

Thus the Lord GOD showed me: Behold, He formed locust swarms at the beginning of the late crop; indeed it was the late crop after the king's mowings. And so it was, when they had finished eating the grass of the land, that I said:"O Lord GOD, forgive, I pray! Oh, that Jacob may stand, For he is small!" So the LORD relented concerning this. "It shall not be," said the LORD.

April 20, 1982

To Henry Willet from Jim Thompson regarding the locust in the Sanctuary Old Testament Window-

"Keep the locust, but don't let it be too overpowering."

THE LOCUST

The mention of the locust in the book of Amos is part of at least four visions of the great prophet, each one a commentary on the disobedience of the people of Israel and the ensuing judgment of God on the nation. Like a good attorney, Amos has constructed a solid, airtight case against Israel. The nations surrounding Israel have behaved poorly and Israel has done no better. Instead of standing apart from the world in righteousness and obedience, Israel has become alarming like the other nations. Their greatest transgressions include oppression of the poor, the accumulation of wealth at the expense of the nation's character, and corruption of the worship of God. Now, having heard the evidence, God speaks in judgment ("The Lord roars from Zion").

The use of the locust in judgment is no surprise to those who read Amos for the first time. They were quite familiar with the locust. Locusts were one of the plagues that prompted Pharaoh to release Israel from slavery in Egypt. The lawgiver in Deuteronomy had predicted that locusts would destroy the crops of Israel when the nation became disobedient, and King Solomon promised the same consequence at the dedication of the temple in Jerusalem. In total, at least twenty times the writers of the Old Testament connected locusts and destruction of crops with God's judgment of Israel. To an agrarian culture, destruction of the crops meant certain death.

Even though Amos is able to delay the wrath of God for a time with a passionate intercession, the judgment will come. It will come as surely as the plumb line reveals a defect and as surely as a basket of summer fruit will wither.

Of what value, then, is the use of the locust in the judgment of Israel to the modern reader? Great, great value! We are reminded that the locust, like everything else in creation, is in the hands of God. It becomes a tool through which the people will be chastised, punished, and finally redeemed. While the locust, as negative an image as it is, symbolized wrath and judgment, the final words from God are always grace and reconciliation. The book of Amos ends not with the judgment of God and the separation of God from God's people, but with a promise that the people of Israel will be called back home, breaches will be repaired, and "...they shall plant vineyards... and make gardens."

The lowly, destructive locust is a tool for the redemption of God's people. We Christian people have read ahead and we understand the symbolism. We know that a lowly, destructive cross will be used at Calvary to bring about the redemption of the world. We are able, then, to face every cross in our own lives, every locust, and every other calamity with confidence and hope in the realization that God can use this difficult moment, too, to bring about God's justice and reconciliation.

Readers who put down the book of Amos without finishing it, who hear only judgment and separation, do not hear the final words of reconciliation and homecoming. In the same way, Christians who succumb to fear and anxiety on Good Friday, who see only death and darkness and who walk away, miss the joy and rebirth of Easter morning. The locust and the cross are mere tools, tools that God uses to bring about the redemption and fullness of the world.

Dr. Sam R. Matthews

Marietta, Georgia

Daniel and the Lions

Daniel 6:22

"My God sent his angel and he shut the mouths of the lions. They have not hurt me, because I was found innocent in his sight. Nor have I ever done any wrong before you, O king."

DANIEL

The eastern window includes a picture of the biblical character Daniel, between two lions. Since we were children we've heard the story of Daniel in the lion's den, but what does Daniel's story offer us today. We're not threatened by lions, are we?

What do you remember about Daniel? Daniel was placed in the lion's den by a reluctant King Darius because Daniel had violated a thirty-day injunction which stated that no one was allowed to make a petition to any god or man other than to the king. Daniel was set up by the ruling commissioners and satraps who found him continuing to pray to God. King Darius had no choice but to throw Daniel into the lion's den.

How was Daniel able to survive an entire night at the disposal of hungry lions? Daniel was not just lucky. Daniel was *prepared*. Daniel made a decision long ago to be faithful to God and to live a life pleasing to Him. It is no accident that Daniel was able to walk out of the lion's den completely unharmed. *He had lived a superb life in the eyes of God.*

What does the book of Daniel tell us about the sort of life Daniel lived? First, he was *disciplined*. Chapter 1 tells us that Daniel, while held in captivity by Babylonian king Nebuchadnezzar, refused the king's rich food and wine and asked for vegetables and water "...that he might not defile himself," (Daniel 1:8). This proved to be a good choice; for Daniel *and* his three friends, Shadrach, Meshach, and Abednego, were stronger in appearance than those youths who ate the king's choice foods. As a result, "God gave them knowledge and intelligence in every branch of literature and wisdom; Daniel even understood all kinds of visions and dreams," (Daniel1:17).

Second, Daniel had a *healthy prayer life*. He understood the power of prayer and knew that through prayer he would be better able to discern how God wanted him to handle the pressures of his daily living. God gave Daniel the gift of being able to interpret King Nebuchadnezzar's dreams which brought Daniel greater power in the King's court.

Third, Daniel *exercised his faith even in difficult circumstances*. Daniel knew that he would be in trouble for praying to God during the thirty-day injunction signed by King Darius. He did it anyway. Daniel's actions were not based on fears or outcomes. Daniel had faith in God, and he knew that following God's precepts were most important no matter what might happen in the future. Daniel had faith that God would prevail.

Another interesting side of this story is how King Darius reacted to his own ruling. You see, Daniel continued to stand out among his fellow commissioners. Daniel Chapter 6 tells us that King Darius had plans to appoint Daniel leader over his entire kingdom. Imagine how the other commissioners felt about this! They were not happy, and this led to the set up of Daniel and his being thrown into the lions' den.

Our picture of Daniel on the eastern window exudes peace. Notice his hands, relaxed and floating peacefully above the heads of the two lions. The lions do not show aggression or ferocity. The picture portrays a scene of order and peace, exhibiting a sense that not only is Daniel in control and confident, but that the whole environment is at peace with the creator. The story told in Daniel is replete with anxiety - by kings and satraps and commissioners and wise men, but no anxiety appears on the face of Daniel at this most perilous time. It almost appears as if Daniel is among domestic pets, so at peace is the scene. And what of King Darius, who issued what many thought was a death sentence, but who was so drawn to Daniel's confidence and serenity and to the source of Daniel's power - that he rushed to the den - after a sleepless night - hoping that this special Daniel was still alive? King Darius sensed the power of the one true creator God and rejoiced and praised that God in the morning light.

Thankfully, punishment by being thrown into a lion's den has long sense vanished from the risks we face. But we still face lions - lions of addiction, or stress, or divorce, or our own sense of failure. Might it still be - after all these ages, that discipline, and prayer, and courage over fear in the face of troubles, are gifts given by the eternal God intended for our peace, and his glory? Daniel watches down, as we worship, inviting us into that life of peace.

Lora & Jody Cooley

Isaiah-The Suffering Servant

Isaiah 53: 5

But he was wounded for our transgressions, he was bruised for our iniquities; upon him was the chastisement that made us whole, and with his stripes we are healed.

Isaiah 53:12

Therefore I will divide him a portion with the great, and he shall divide the spoil with the strong; because he poured out his soul to death, and was numbered with the transgressors; yet he bore the sin of many, and made intercession for the transgressors.

Faithfulness: The Highest Form of Success

Of the masses born into this world, only a few are remembered. The words and deeds have stood the test of time. There lived thousands of years ago a man named Isaiah, a Hebrew prophet.

Isaiah's lasting gift to the world was in the form of words. Based on numbers, only a few have read his words and fewer believed what he wrote, and yet, his writings live on. Unbelief and even being unread has not erased his thoughts from the mind of the greatest words passed through the ages.

The words of God, wisdom, were given to the man Isaiah to be shared with others. He became a voice for God to all who believe. The importance of God's words is the key that unlocks the mystery of God. The plan of God for the life of Isaiah was to share God's wisdom with the people of God. Yet his words go beyond and reach all who are seeking and searching the meaning and purpose of life. The thoughts revealed in Isaiah's writings can be found in the New Testament of the Christian's bible. His words were not just for the Hebrew people, but also for the Christian and even the nonbeliever.

Isaiah's words cannot be abolished because God's wisdom cannot be abolished. Isaiah has been remembered not because of the greatness of the man, but because of the greatness of the gift of words he wrote to be shared with all people.

His words bring to all an insight of the God of all. Sin may not be a factor in life for the nonbeliever, but sin, the sins of Israel and Judah were and are in the life and history of God's chosen people. Sin is the battlefield between each of us and our creator. Isaiah's words and the writings of the Bible's New Testament unite to inform us God's thoughts about sin and how we are to cope with the barrier that stands between each of us and our Creator.

We are informed that sin becomes a debt we owe but cannot pay. We are told that each comes under the judgment of God. Isaiah, the voice of God, makes it vividly clear that each of us has become disobedient to the laws of God. For this disobedience the judgment of God falls upon us. We are made aware of our wrong and even given God's future plans for giving us Hope when we cannot see hope as an option.

Isaiah expressed that Hope is on the way. He writes, "For to us a child is born, to us a son is given, and the government will be on his shoulders. And he will be called Wonderful Counselor, Mighty God, Everlasting Father, Prince of Peace."

What Isaiah is saying is that sin takes us away from God, but there is coming an awakening to a road that leads us home. We call this road Jesus and the road home begins at the cross. As sin leads us away, God, through Jesus, built a road that takes us home.

Many are born into this world, but only a few are remembered. Isaiah was such a man, not because of his greatness, but he is remembered because of the words and hope given him to be shared with a very sin filled world.

Each of us is given, by God, the gift of listening. It is the use of this gift that has preserved our remembrance of this man. God speaks in varying ways. Our problem is our failure to listen. But He speaks to each of us. What a different world it would be if we use this gift. Isaiah used his gift and was mostly mocked. Yet in spite of this unbelief and mockery his writings and thoughts continue to exist.

If his words are not from God why and how have they withstood the test of time? Yet, they have and shall continue. There will be doubters until the end of time, but his words and thoughts shall prevail.

The world in Isaiah's day was not as different from the world of today as we might expect. Or course, there are differences, but when we look at the problems of Isaiah's day with our time, his words become as relevant for us of today as they were when first written and spoken.

God spoke and Isaiah listened, but God's Chosen People would not listen. Both the leadership of Israel and the people of Jerusalem themselves became more and more withdrawn, putting the God that created aside. No longer following the will of God, because they chose to follow rebellious pride refusing to be faithful to God and His will for His people.

Isaiah became more and more aware of the moral evil that prevailed throughout the nation. God informed Isaiah, that He was weary of them and of those who honored him with their lips, while their hearts were far from Him. Isaiah was made to know the feeling of God as it applied to their morally unclean minds, their sexuality and their materialism.

What Yahweh demanded of them was that they should become clean; that they should cease to do evil; and learn to do right. God's people could not even distinguish any more between good and evil. What He saw and relayed to Isaiah is as current as the new on TV today. Isn't it interesting he could have written for us of today and not changed his text at all? The people ignored his words as we would today. The nation of Judah ceased to exist because they would not listen and ignored the advice. Could it be the way of Judah might become the way of our nation?

Isaiah his God given thoughts have stood the test of time for two reasons – they were God's words and they were truthful words. So Isaiah shall always be remembered because he was called to be the voice of God to share the word and the truth.

When we pass Isaiah's window, it would be well for us to pause and remember that the image depicted there is a man of God who speaks to one and all and so shall it be to the end of time.

Isaiah may not have been successful as the world defines success. However, Isaiah's image reminds us that God calls us not to be successful but to be faithful. Isaiah glorified his God by being faithful to his call to be God's prophet.

Rev. Jack E. Summers
Methodist Minister
North GA Conference (1964 – 2013)

Jonah and the Whale

Jonah 1:17

Now the LORD had prepared a great fish to swallow up Jonah. And Jonah was in the belly of the fish three days and three nights.

.

Jonah 2:10

And the LORD commanded the fish, and it vomited Jonah onto dry land.

Jonah, Jesus, The Prodigal Son, and Me

The Bible was written over several thousand years, yet hidden within its pages are subtle signs that point to a single figure in time, namely Jesus. All roads, no matter how crooked, have always pointed to him. The story of Jonah is no different. Jesus' fingerprints can be seen from beginning to end. For many, this account has largely been relegated to a children's story. Scholars have debated whether or not this story is factual. There are some who believe that it was meant to be interpreted only figuratively. Regardless of your position, this story has much to teach us about God, ourselves, and our nation.

Jonah was a prophet instructed by God to proclaim a message of repentance to the people of Nineveh. Instead of obeying God, Jonah ran in the opposite direction. A series of unfortunate events followed him. He fled to sea and was caught in a great storm. Then the sailors of the ship threw him overboard where he almost perished. Shortly thereafter, he was swallowed by a great whale and carried back to dry land. From there, Jonah walked to Nineveh to complete the assignment which he had been given. *"Jonah started into the city…and he cried out, 'Just forty days more and Nineveh will be overthrown!'"* (Jonah 3:4). To this message, *"The people of Nineveh believed God. They proclaimed a fast and put on mourning clothes, from the greatest of them to the least significant"* (Jonah 3:5). Then *"God saw what they were doing, that they had ceased their evil behavior, and (he) stopped planning to destroy them"* (Jonah 3:10). Jonah was not pleased that the people of Nineveh had repented or that God had forgiven them. Jonah had hoped that God would destroy them. The story concludes with Jonah expressing his anger towards God. In the final chapter, Jonah states on two separate occasions that he would have rather died than witness the pardoning of the Ninevites.

Jonah's story is referenced twice by Jesus. The first reference comes from Matthew 12:40. It reads, *"For just as Jonah was in the belly of the great fish for three days and three nights, so the Son of Man will be in the heart of the earth for three days and three nights."* The second comes from Luke 11:29-30. It reads, *"This generation is a wicked generation. It demands a sign, yet no sign will be given to it except the sign of Jonah. For just as Jonah became a sign to the Ninevites, so also the Son of Man will be to this generation."* In many ways, Jonah's story was a foreshadowing of his own. Like Jonah, Jesus was sent to a people who desperately needed repentance. Judgment was coming to Israel in the form of the Roman Empire. They needed to repent and turn back to God or face the penalty of their sinful ways. Like Jonah, Jesus' message was for both the Israelites and the Gentiles. Like Jonah, Jesus spent three days dead to this world before returning to complete his task. However, from here, the similarities between Jesus and Jonah come to an end. Jesus came to this world out of love. Jonah acted for selfish reasons. In many ways, Jonah's story mirrors one of Jesus' most beloved parables. In fact, Jesus might have had this story in mind when he told it. It is the parable of The Prodigal Son. In this version of this story, God plays the father, Jonah plays the older son, and the Ninevites play the part of the younger son.

In the parable of the Prodigal Son, Jesus reveals God's nature to us through the father figure. He is portrayed as being loving, merciful, and patient towards both of his children. In a similar manner, God reveals some of these same characteristics in the story of Jonah. His love and grace are displayed through the act of sending Jonah to warn the people of Nineveh. He didn't have to do this but he chose to send Jonah to a people who *"couldn't tell their right hand from their left"* (Jonah 4:11). Next, he displayed mercy by readily forgiving the Ninevites when they repented. He displayed patience with Jonah, even though Jonah had disobeyed and grown angry with him. Finally, he displayed his power. He created a storm and then calmed it. He commanded a whale to carry Jonah back to dry land. He used Jonah, an unwilling participant, to deliver his message. Then he changed the course of human history by delaying the instrument of his wrath towards Nineveh, namely the invasion of the Babylonian army.

Jonah is a classic example of the older son. The older son was angry and resentful towards his father for taking back his younger brother. His pride had gotten in the way of their relationship. As a result, he alienated himself from both his father and brother. He refused to go to the party, shaming himself and his father in the process. In Jonah's story, a similar situation occurs between Jonah and God. Jonah was angry and resentful towards God for asking him to go to Nineveh. His personal and national pride had gotten in the way of his relationship with God. Like most Israelites, he believed that they were God's chosen people. God had formed his covenants with them. Therefore, his blessings should only be for them. In addition, like most Israelites, he believed that God would protect them by destroying their enemies. I can only imagine how Jonah must have felt when God gave him the job of warning the Ninevites. The Ninevites were foreigners, not God's chosen people. Even worse, they were mortal enemies of the Israelites. This was so contrary to everything that Jonah believed that he had trouble accepting it. In his heart, this was not what he desired. He didn't want any part in the Ninevites' redemption. He would have rather seen them destroyed. In fact, his desire to see his enemies perish was so great that he would have rather died himself. Like the older brother, his pride had gotten in the way. When God's plan didn't align with his own, he rebelled. When forced to comply, his anger and resentment towards God only grew. Like the older son, Jonah's story ends with him sitting outside the party at odds with both God and the Ninevites.

The Ninevites played the role of the prodigal son in this story. They were a lost people, even though they didn't know it. They had not been blessed with the same knowledge as the Israelites. They had not been given God's commandments. Thus, they had no knowledge of his statues or ways. They were like children without parents. They had drifted off course and didn't know it. Over time, their wickedness only worsened. At the time of this story, God's patience with their behavior had reached its limit. Their judgment was at hand. Then God sent Jonah into their lives with one final message: repent or be destroyed. In an amazing fashion, *"the people of Nineveh believed God. They proclaimed a fast and put on mourning clothes, from the greatest of them to the least significant"* (Jonah 3:5). Then the king gave this decree: *"Let everyone turn from his evil ways and from the violence that is in his hands. Who knows? God may turn and relent and turn from his fierce anger, so that we may not perish"* (Jonah 3:8-9). When they heard Jonah's message, they took it to heart and repented. They realized that continuing in the same manner would only lead to their destruction, so they left their sinful ways. In the story of the Prodigal Son, the younger son had a similar moment of self-realization. He realized that he had deviated away from the life that his father had taught him to live. He had slowly drifted from living the good life to living a life of self-indulgence to finally living a life of self-preservation. In this moment, he had to make a choice...continue in his current self-defeating path or make a change for the better. Choosing the latter, he left his sin-ridden swine pen and began the long journey back home.

On an individual level, the story of Jonah still has a great deal to teach us. Each character has a story within itself which can be used to better understand our relationship with God. From the very beginning, we see that it is God who reaches out to us, not the other way around. God is always present, trying to make himself known. To Jonah, God revealed the full spectrum of being. The story begins with God's judgment, anger, and wrath. Then it flows into his love before concluding with a display of his mercy and forgiveness. We must never forget that God is the sum of all of his characteristics. We cannot pick and choose the attributes that we like and ignore the ones that we don't such as his judgment, anger, and wraith. God is holy and pure, and he will not tolerate sin forever. Wrongs must be made right, either in this age or in the one to come. It is for this very reason that Jesus was sent. He became an atoning sacrifice for our sins. God's wrath was laid upon him. Those who have repented and claimed this free gift are spared because God has forgiven them. Sadly, those who have rejected Jesus will one day face the sobering reality that their condemnation still remains.

In the book entitled Prodigal God, the author, Timothy Keller, enlightens the reader to the reality that in many ways we respond to God by either playing the role of the younger or older son. Ironically, the motivation for both responses is the same even though the behaviors are quite different. He writes, "The hearts of the two brothers were the same. Both sons resented their father's authority and sought ways of getting out from under it. They wanted to get into a position in which they could tell the father what to do. Each one, in other words, rebelled – but one did so by being very bad and the other by being extremely good. Both were alienated from the father's heart; both were lost sons. Neither son loved the father for himself. They both were using the father for their own self-centered ends rather than loving, enjoying, and serving him for his own sake." As previously mentioned, Jonah exemplified the older brother. Through him, we learn that there is no place in the Christian's heart for selfishness because it only leads to other problems such as pride, judgment, anger, and resentment. Together, these problems will coalesce, creating a sense of self-righteousness that only undermines our relationship with God.

In comparison to the older brother, the Ninevites existed on the other end of the spectrum. They acted selfishly but not for self-righteous reasons. Their selfishness was more carnal in nature. Sin had overcome them. It had become their master. As a result, they allowed it to lead them down the age old path heading to destruction. There are two levels in which the story of the Ninevites should be viewed. The first is on an individual level. As Christians, this story teaches us that we have an obligation to warn our neighbors who are traveling down the wrong path. Jesus commanded us to be the light of the world. Without it, they may never find the way home. The second level in which this story should be viewed is a national one. In the Old Testament, there a several occasions where God's wrath was poured upon nations that did not heed his warnings. The Ninevites were unique in the fact that they were the only nation that did respond. As Christians, this story teaches us that we have a responsibility to warn our country if it ever gets off course. If we don't, then we put our country at risk for receiving a similar fate.

On a personal note, I have seen myself on both ends of this spectrum. I have been in both sets of shoes. For years, I was the prodigal son. I ran from God, living a sin-filled life. Fortunately, he never gave up on me. Through the witnesses of others, he helped me find my way back home. Years later, after returning to God, I fell into the trap of becoming the older brother. My motivation for loving God became a selfish one. Today, I am afraid that I still alternate between the two but thank God I am able to discern much quicker when I have drifted to one side or the other. Now I try to walk the narrow path as I love God while serving his purposes and not my own. I try to shed his light into a world that desperately needs to hear the message of his love. I fear for those who don't know him, so I try to warn them of the pitfalls that lay ahead. In a similar way, I fear for our country. I am afraid that we are taking the path of the Ninevites, and without a change, our future is in jeopardy. Several years ago, God spoke to my heart. He warned me that our future is filled with trouble. We have fallen as a nation. Christian idealism has waned, and in its place, wickedness has begun to abound. The change has occurred so gradually that its acuity has not been felt by the church. The world has demanded tolerance, and I am afraid that we have succumbed to it. It has become our anesthetic, and so while we slumber, our morality has been chipped away one stroke at a time. Like the Ninevites, our day of judgment is at hand. The real question is will we respond? It is my hope that Christians across our country will wake up and begin fighting for what is right. For years, I have held this burden in my heart. Like Jonah, I didn't want to share it. Figuratively speaking, you might say that I ran from God. However, I have come to realize that there is nowhere to hide, for just when I thought that I had escaped, a whale entered into my life, gobbled me up, spit me out, and then asked me to write a fish tale about Jonah and myself.

Brad Pierce

Chapter Nine-The Sermon

From

Moby Dick by Herman Melville

Father Mapple rose, and in a mild voice of unassuming authority ordered the scattered people to condense. "Starboard gangway, there! side away to larboard--larboard gangway to starboard! Midships! Midships!"

There was a low rumbling of heavy sea-boots among the benches, and a still slighter shuffling of women's shoes, and all was quiet again, and every eye on the preacher.

He paused a little; then kneeling in the pulpit's bows, folded his large brown hands across his chest, uplifted his closed eyes, and offered a prayer so deeply devout that he seemed kneeling and praying at the bottom of the sea.

This ended, in prolonged solemn tones, like the continual tolling of a bell in a ship that is foundering at sea in a fog--in such tones he commenced reading the following hymn; but changing his manner towards the concluding stanzas, burst forth with a pealing exultation and joy--

"The ribs and terrors in the whale,
Arched over me a dismal gloom,
While all God's sun-lit waves rolled by,
And lift me deepening down to doom.

"I saw the opening maw of hell,
With endless pains and sorrows there;
Which none but they that feel can tell--
Oh, I was plunging to despair.

"In black distress, I called my God,
When I could scarce believe him mine,
He bowed his ear to my complaints--
No more the whale did me confine.

"With speed he flew to my relief,
As on a radiant dolphin borne;
Awful, yet bright, as lightning shone
The face of my Deliverer God.

*"My song for ever shall record
That terrible, that joyful hour;
I give the glory to my God,
His all the mercy and the power.*

Nearly all joined in singing this hymn, which swelled high above the howling of the storm. A brief pause ensued; the preacher slowly turned over the leaves of the Bible, and at last, folding his hand down upon the proper page, said: "Beloved shipmates, clinch the last verse of the first chapter of Jonah--'And God had prepared a great fish to swallow up Jonah.'"

"Shipmates, this book, containing only four chapters--four yarns--is one of the smallest strands in the mighty cable of the Scriptures. Yet what depths of the soul does Jonah's deep sea line sound! What a pregnant lesson to us is this prophet! What a noble thing is that canticle in the fish's belly! How billow-like and boisterously grand! We feel the floods surging over us; we sound with him to the kelpy bottom of the waters; sea-weed and all the slime of the sea is about us! But WHAT is this lesson that the book of Jonah teaches? Shipmates, it is a two-stranded lesson; a lesson to us all as sinful men, and a lesson to me as a pilot of the living God. As sinful men, it is a lesson to us all, because it is a story of the sin, hard-heartedness, suddenly awakened fears, the swift punishment, repentance, prayers, and finally the deliverance and joy of Jonah. As with all sinners among men, the sin of this son of Amittai was in his willful disobedience of the command of God--never mind now what that command was, or how conveyed--which he found a hard command. But all the things that God would have us do are hard for us to do--remember that--and hence, he oftener commands us than endeavors to persuade. And if we obey God, we must disobey ourselves; and it is in this disobeying ourselves, wherein the hardness of obeying God consists.

"With this sin of disobedience in him, Jonah still further flouts at God, by seeking to flee from Him. He thinks that a ship made by men will carry him into countries where God does not reign, but only the Captains of this earth. He skulks about the wharves of Joppa, and seeks a ship that's bound for Tarshish. There lurks, perhaps, a hitherto unheeded meaning here. By all accounts Tarshish could have been no other city than the modern Cadiz. That's the opinion of learned men. And where is Cadiz, shipmates? Cadiz is in Spain; as far by water, from Joppa, as Jonah could possibly have sailed in those ancient days, when the Atlantic was an almost unknown sea. Because Joppa, the modern Jaffa, shipmates, is on the most easterly coast of the Mediterranean, the Syrian; and Tarshish or Cadiz more than two thousand miles to the westward from that, just outside the Straits of Gibraltar. See ye not then, shipmates, that Jonah sought to flee world-wide from God? Miserable man! Oh! Most contemptible and worthy of all scorn; with slouched hat and guilty eye, skulking from his God; prowling among the shipping like a vile burglar hastening to cross the seas. So disordered, self-condemning is his look, that had there been policemen in those days, Jonah, on the mere suspicion of something wrong, had been arrested ere he touched a deck. How plainly he's a fugitive! No baggage, not a hat-box, valise, or carpet-bag,--no friends accompany him to the wharf with their adieux. At last, after much dodging search, he finds the Tarshish ship receiving the last items of her cargo; and as he steps on board to see its Captain in the cabin, all the sailors for the moment desist from hoisting

in the goods, to mark the stranger's evil eye. Jonah sees this; but in vain he tries to look all ease and confidence; in vain essays his wretched smile. Strong intuitions of the man assure the mariners he can be no innocent. In their gamesome but still serious way, one whispers to the other--"Jack, he's robbed a widow;" or, "Joe, do you mark him; he's a bigamist;" or, "Harry lad, I guess he's the adulterer that broke jail in old Gomorrah, or belike, one of the missing murderers from Sodom." Another runs to read the bill that's stuck against the spile upon the wharf to which the ship is moored, offering five hundred gold coins for the apprehension of a parricide, and containing a description of his person. He reads, and looks from Jonah to the bill; while all his sympathetic shipmates now crowd round Jonah, prepared to lay their hands upon him. Frighted Jonah trembles, and summoning all his boldness to his face, only looks so much the more a coward. He will not confess himself suspected; but that itself is strong suspicion. So he makes the best of it; and when the sailors find him not to be the man that is advertised, they let him pass, and he descends into the cabin.

"'Who's there?' cries the Captain at his busy desk, hurriedly making out his papers for the Customs--'Who's there?' Oh! how that harmless question mangles Jonah! For the instant he almost turns to flee again. But he rallies. 'I seek a passage in this ship to Tarshish; how soon sail ye, sir?' Thus far the busy Captain had not looked up to Jonah, though the man now stands before him; but no sooner does he hear that hollow voice, than he darts a scrutinizing glance. 'We sail with the next coming tide,' at last he slowly answered, still intently eyeing him. 'No sooner, sir?'--'Soon enough for any honest man that goes a passenger.' Ha! Jonah, that's another stab. But he swiftly calls away the Captain from that scent. 'I'll sail with ye,'--he says,-- 'the passage money how much is that?--I'll pay now.' For it is particularly written, shipmates, as if it were a thing not to be overlooked in this history, 'that he paid the fare thereof' ere the craft did sail. And taken with the context, this is full of meaning.

"Now Jonah's Captain, shipmates, was one whose discernment detects crime in any, but whose cupidity exposes it only in the penniless. In this world, shipmates, sin that pays its way can travel freely, and without a passport; whereas Virtue, if a pauper, is stopped at all frontiers. So Jonah's Captain prepares to test the length of Jonah's purse, ere he judge him openly. He charges him thrice the usual sum; and it's assented to. Then the Captain knows that Jonah is a fugitive; but at the same time resolves to help a flight that paves its rear with gold. Yet when Jonah fairly takes out his purse, prudent suspicions still molest the Captain. He rings every coin to find a counterfeit. Not a forger, any way, he mutters; and Jonah is put down for his passage. 'Point out my state-room, Sir,' says Jonah now, 'I'm travel-weary; I need sleep.' 'Thou lookest like it,' says the Captain, 'there's thy room.' Jonah enters, and would lock the door, but the lock contains no key. Hearing him foolishly fumbling there, the Captain laughs lowly to himself, and mutters something about the doors of convicts' cells being never allowed to be locked within. All dressed and dusty as he is, Jonah throws himself into his berth, and finds the little state-room ceiling almost resting on his forehead. The air is close, and Jonah gasps. Then, in that contracted hole, sunk, too, beneath the ship's water-line, Jonah feels the heralding presentiment of that stifling hour, when the whale shall hold him in the smallest of his bowels' wards.

"Screwed at its axis against the side, a swinging lamp slightly oscillates in Jonah's room; and the ship, heeling over towards the wharf with the weight of the last bales received, the lamp, flame and all, though in slight motion, still maintains a permanent obliquity with reference to the room; though, in truth, infallibly straight itself, it but made obvious the false, lying levels among which it hung. The lamp alarms and frightens Jonah; as lying in his berth his tormented eyes roll round the place, and this thus far successful fugitive finds no refuge for his restless glance. But that contradiction in the lamp more and more appals him. The floor, the ceiling, and the side, are all awry. 'Oh! so my conscience hangs in me!' he groans, 'straight upwards, so it burns; but the chambers of my soul are all in crookedness!'

"Like one who after a night of drunken revelry hies to his bed, still reeling, but with conscience yet pricking him, as the plungings of the Roman race-horse but so much the more strike his steel tags into him; as one who in that miserable plight still turns and turns in giddy anguish, praying God for annihilation until the fit be passed; and at last amid the whirl of woe he feels, a deep stupor steals over him, as over the man who bleeds to death, for conscience is the wound, and there's naught to staunch it; so, after sore wrestlings in his berth, Jonah's prodigy of ponderous misery drags him drowning down to sleep.

"And now the time of tide has come; the ship casts off her cables; and from the deserted wharf the uncheered ship for Tarshish, all careening, glides to sea. That ship, my friends, was the first of recorded smugglers! the contraband was Jonah. But the sea rebels; he will not bear the wicked burden. A dreadful storm comes on, the ship is like to break. But now when the boatswain calls all hands to lighten her; when boxes, bales, and jars are clattering overboard; when the wind is shrieking, and the men are yelling, and every plank thunders with trampling feet right over Jonah's head; in all this raging tumult, Jonah sleeps his hideous sleep. He sees no black sky and raging sea, feels not the reeling timbers, and little hears he or heeds he the far rush of the mighty whale, which even now with open mouth is cleaving the seas after him. Aye, shipmates, Jonah was gone down into the sides of the ship--a berth in the cabin as I have taken it, and was fast asleep. But the frightened master comes to him, and shrieks in his dead ear, 'What meanest thou, O, sleeper! arise!' Startled from his lethargy by that direful cry, Jonah staggers to his feet, and stumbling to the deck, grasps a shroud, to look out upon the sea. But at that moment he is sprung upon by a panther billow leaping over the bulwarks. Wave after wave thus leaps into the ship, and finding no speedy vent runs roaring fore and aft, till the mariners come nigh to drowning while yet afloat. And ever, as the white moon shows her affrighted face from the steep gullies in the blackness overhead, aghast Jonah sees the rearing bowsprit pointing high upward, but soon beat downward again towards the tormented deep.

"Terrors upon terrors run shouting through his soul. In all his cringing attitudes, the God-fugitive is now too plainly known. The sailors mark him; more and more certain grow their suspicions of him, and at last, fully to test the truth, by referring the whole matter to high Heaven, they fall to casting lots, to see for whose cause this great tempest was upon them. The lot is Jonah's; that discovered, then how furiously they mob him with their questions. 'What is thine occupation? Whence comest thou? Thy country? What people? But mark now, my shipmates, the behavior of poor Jonah. The eager mariners but ask him who he is, and where from; whereas, they not only *receive an answer to those questions, but likewise another answer to a question not put by them, but the unsolicited answer is forced from Jonah by the hard hand of God that is upon him.*

"'I am a Hebrew,' he cries--and then--'I fear the Lord the God of Heaven who hath made the sea and the dry land!' Fear him, O Jonah? Aye, well mightest thou fear the Lord God THEN! Straightway, he now goes on to make a full confession; whereupon the mariners became more and more appalled, but still are pitiful. For when Jonah, not yet supplicating God for mercy, since he but too well knew the darkness of his deserts,--when wretched Jonah cries out to them to take him and cast him forth into the sea, for he knew that for HIS sake this great tempest was upon them; they mercifully turn from him, and seek by other means to save the ship. But all in vain; the indignant gale howls louder; then, with one hand raised invokingly to God, with the other they not unreluctantly lay hold of Jonah.

"And now behold Jonah taken up as an anchor and dropped into the sea; when instantly an oily calmness floats out from the east, and the sea is still, as Jonah carries down the gale with him, leaving smooth water behind. He goes down in the whirling heart of such a masterless commotion that he scarce heeds the moment when he drops seething into the yawning jaws awaiting him; and the whale shoots-to all his ivory teeth, like so many white bolts, upon his prison. Then Jonah prayed unto the Lord out of the fish's belly. But observe his prayer, and learn a weighty lesson. For sinful as he is, Jonah does not weep and wail for direct deliverance. He feels that his dreadful punishment is just. He leaves all his deliverance to God, contenting himself with this, that spite of all his pains and pangs, he will still look towards His holy temple. And here, shipmates, is true and faithful repentance; not clamorous for pardon, but grateful for punishment. And how pleasing to God was this conduct in Jonah, is shown in the eventual deliverance of him from the sea and the whale. Shipmates, I do not place Jonah before you to be copied for his sin but I do place him before you as a model for repentance. Sin not; but if you do, take heed to repent of it like Jonah."

While he was speaking these words, the howling of the shrieking, slanting storm without seemed to add new power to the preacher, who, when describing Jonah's sea-storm, seemed tossed by a storm himself. His deep chest heaved as with a ground-swell; his tossed arms seemed the warring elements at work; and the thunders that rolled away from off his swarthy brow, and the light leaping from his eye, made all his simple hearers look on him with a quick fear that was strange to them.

There now came a lull in his look, as he silently turned over the leaves of the Book once more; and, at last, standing motionless, with closed eyes, for the moment, seemed communing with God and himself.

But again he leaned over towards the people, and bowing his head lowly, with an aspect of the deepest yet manliest humility, he spake these words:

"Shipmates, God has laid but one hand upon you; both his hands press upon me. I have read ye by what murky light may be mine the lesson that Jonah teaches to all sinners; and therefore to

ye, and still more to me, for I am a greater sinner than ye. And now how gladly would I come down from this mast-head and sit on the hatches there where you sit, and listen as you listen, while some one of you reads ME that other and more awful lesson which Jonah teaches to ME, as a pilot of the living God. How being an anointed pilot-prophet, or speaker of true things, and bidden by the Lord to sound those unwelcome truths in the ears of a wicked Nineveh, Jonah, appalled at the hostility he should raise, fled from his mission, and sought to escape his duty and his God by taking ship at Joppa. But God is everywhere; Tarshish he never reached. As we have seen, God came upon him in the whale, and swallowed him down to living gulfs of doom, and with swift slantings tore him along 'into the midst of the seas,' where the eddying depths sucked him ten thousand fathoms down, and 'the weeds were wrapped about his head,' and all the watery world of woe bowled over him. Yet even then beyond the reach of any plummet--'out of the belly of hell'--when the whale grounded upon the ocean's utmost bones, even then, God heard the engulphed, repenting prophet when he cried. Then God spake unto the fish; and from the shuddering cold and blackness of the sea, the whale came breeching up towards the warm and pleasant sun, and all the delights of air and earth; and 'vomited out Jonah upon the dry land;' when the word of the Lord came a second time; and Jonah, bruised and beaten--his ears, like two sea-shells, still multitudinously murmuring of the ocean--Jonah did the Almighty's bidding. And what was that, shipmates? To preach the Truth to the face of Falsehood! That was it!

"This, shipmates, this is that other lesson; and woe to that pilot of the living God who slights it. Woe to him whom this world charms from Gospel duty! Woe to him who seeks to pour oil upon the waters when God has brewed them into a gale! Woe to him who seeks to please rather than to appal! Woe to him whose good name is more to him than goodness! Woe to him who, in this world, courts not dishonour! Woe to him who would not be true, even though to be false were salvation! Yea, woe to him who, as the great Pilot Paul has it, while preaching to others is himself a castaway!"

He dropped and fell away from himself for a moment; then lifting his face to them again, showed a deep joy in his eyes, as he cried out with a heavenly enthusiasm,--"But oh! shipmates! on the starboard hand of every woe, there is a sure delight; and higher the top of that delight, than the bottom of the woe is deep. Is not the main-truck higher than the kelson is low? Delight is to him--a far, far upward, and inward delight--who against the proud gods and commodores of this earth, ever stands forth his own inexorable self. Delight is to him whose strong arms yet support him, when the ship of this base treacherous world has gone down beneath him. Delight is to him, who gives no quarter in the truth, and kills, burns, and destroys all sin though he pluck it out from under the robes of Senators and Judges. Delight,--top-gallant delight is to him, who acknowledges no law or lord, but the Lord his God, and is only a patriot to heaven. Delight is to him, whom all the waves of the billows of the seas of the boisterous mob can never shake from this sure Keel of the Ages. And eternal delight and deliciousness will be his, who coming to lay him down, can say with his final breath--O Father!--chiefly known to me by Thy rod--mortal or immortal, here I die. I have striven to be Thine, more than to be this world's, or mine own. Yet this is nothing: I leave eternity to Thee; for what is man that he should live out the lifetime of his God?"

He said no more, but slowly waving a benediction, covered his face with his hands, and so remained kneeling, till all the people had departed, and he was left alone in the place.

This story is an Old Testament prophecy of the blessing of the coming Christ would be for all peoples and not just the Jews.

The Rainbow Covenant

Genesis 9: 15-17

And I will remember my covenant, which is between me and you and every living creature of all flesh; and the waters shall no more become a flood to destroy all flesh. And the bow shall be in the cloud; and I will look on it, that I may remember the everlasting covenant between God and every living creature of all flesh that is on the earth. And God said to Noah, This is the token of the covenant, which I have established between me and all the flesh that is on earth.

April 21, 1982

Notes of Henry Willet after conversation with Reverend Thompson

"Make the rainbow more prominent colors."

God's Promise: The Ark and the Rainbow

(Genesis 6:1-9:17)

Bible Truth: God will help you to keep on doing right no matter what others do.

How do you feel when kids around you seem to be having a good time doing something wrong? Does it make you want to join in at times? Sometimes it's very hard to keep on doing right when you seem to be the only one who loves the Lord and wants to please Him. But if you know the Lord Jesus as your Savior, God will help you to keep on doing right, no matter what others do. Noah loved God and stood up for what was right even though everyone else was doing wrong. Noah followed God by building a large boat, called an ark. Many people laughed at Noah, but Noah kept doing what God asked him to do, no matter what others were saying about him. Then the rains came and the earth was flooded. Everything living on the earth was destroyed, but Noah and his family was safe inside the ark. As a promise to Noah and to all people, God put a rainbow in the sky as a sign that He would never again flood the entire earth. God always keeps his promises. If you know Jesus as your Savior, God has promised to help you to keep on doing right no matter what others do. Many people choose to do wrong, just as they did in Noah's time, but you can do the right thing by praying to God asking Him to help you make good choices. God will give you the strength to not give up, no matter what! Look at the picture of the stained glass ark and rainbow to remind yourself of God's wonderful promises!

Prayer: Dear God, thank you for keeping your promises. Thank you for helping me make good choices so that I can do what is right, no matter what! Amen.

Rebecca Benson

Director of Children Ministries

"But Noah found grace in the eyes of the Lord." –Genesis 6:5-8

Little Noah

The Story of Noah and the Ark has been told as a children's story for years. Its literal message explained that God was displeased with how corrupt man and the world had become. He decided to destroy all the inhabitants of Earth except for Noah and his family who had found "grace before the eyes of God." (Gen. 6:5-8) Noah is said to have been 600 years old when God instructed him to build the ark and gather two kinds of every animal on board with him and his family. The rains came and floods covered the Earth for 150 days. After the waters receded, Noah sent forth a dove that later returned with an olive branch signifying there was dry ground. God then blessed Noah and his sons saying to them, "Be fruitful and multiply." (Gen.9:1)

Although I taught this story in Sunday School to children who readily accepted my lesson without question, I was the one who had questions. I tried to overlook the specifics of building an ark to house the animals and the logistics of feeding all the animals. I wasn't yet able to see a deeper message other than the importance of pleasing God which was a pretty hefty undertaking. Was I behaving as "one" who could possibly find favor in God's eyes? What if He called me, would I be willing to say yes, as solidly as Noah did?

Years later I would come upon a paper written by my son, one he never asked me to proofread, that challenged the reader to question if Moses and the Ten Plagues was credible due to the absence of scientific evidence to verify this religious story. Here I was again, faced with my child presenting questions about a story in the Bible from a literal standpoint. Were the Ten Plagues a show of mighty preeminence or were they just the repercussions of one of the most explosive volcanic eruptions in historic times? Was I to challenge the story of Noah and the Ark because the remains of the Ark had not been found on the "mountains of Ararat?"

Trying to interpret the story of Noah or any scripture from a literal perspective leaves one with more questions than answers. However, we know that just as children's stories are written to teach a lesson, the scriptures were written to serve as a guide throughout our journey of spiritual development. Franciscan priest and author, Fr. Richard Rohr points out, "the only language available to religion is metaphor. There's no other language possible. How do you talk about transcendent, eternal, spiritual things? You have to find metaphorical words that approximate the reality." So if we begin with the understanding that the Bible is a book of spiritual instruction, what symbolic meaning might Noah have for us?

As I look at the stained glass window of Noah, I am taken with how small he is in relation to the boat, the dove and the waves; as small as a seed. What if Noah represents the seed of the Divine soul that is planted in each of us? Meister Eckhart calls this combustion the God-spark. What if Noah represents the tiny bit of God that is placed in all of us from the beginning? Perhaps the story of the Ark is calling each one of us to discover our inner-Noah.

How does one go about discovering their small, inner-Noah? As with many stories in the Bible, we will need to learn how to be still, listen and reply to the calling as Noah did. It appears we will also have to learn how to build our ark and if Noah's age has any implication upon the length of time this might take we will discern that the building process could take us a lifetime! In his book *Falling Upward: Spirituality for the Two Halves of Life*, Richard Rohr postures that "the first half of life is spent building our container, our identity, or perhaps we could call it, our ark. It is what life calls us to do: go to school, secure a job, start a family, become a leader in the community and find a financial planner to help us increase the odds of a comfortable retirement. It is then that the rains come, or perhaps it is a flood, that pushes us towards the realization that all the stuff we pretend to be, the titles, roles and labels placed upon us by society, the taking of our college degree as who we are, is not the full journey." This is where I think God desires for us to answer His call to find our True Self, our inner-Noah, and let go of the False Self or ego that measures, evaluates and labels. God sees each one of us as worthy of being called, just like Noah. I have read that it is by mystery or grace that this call occurs and the desire to be less filled with ourselves, with our idealized role or self-made identity, is placed before us to help us encounter Him within us. Perhaps the flood symbolizes the cleansing process that must begin in order for us to unearth the contents of our ark. As we persistently disturb the earth, the divine seed lies waiting to be transformed.

From now on when I see little Noah in the stained glass, I will think of God asking each one of us to be brave and daring enough to seek out and endure the floods that can wash away our small and petty selves. May we have the patience to wait for our dove to return, land on dry ground and emerge from the ark in our Noah-likeness. May we be fruitful and multiply as we celebrate our inner-Noah each day by asking God to show us what we are to do and that He may give us the strength and willingness to carry it out.

Valerie Butts

NEW TESTAMENT SIDE

THE LIFE OF JESUS

EARLY LIFE OF JESUS   ASCENSION OF JESUS   MINISTRIES

Mathew 2:9-10

After hearing the king, they went their way; and the star, which they had seen in the east, went on before them until it came and stood over the place where the Child was. When they saw the star, they rejoiced exceedingly with great joy....

Baby Jesus in the Manger under the Star of Bethlehem

Luke 2:7

And she brought forth her firstborn Son, and wrapped Him in swaddling cloths, and laid Him in a manger, because there was no room for them in the inn.

Mathew 2:2

Saying, Where is he that is born King of the Jews? For we have seen his star in the east, and are come to worship him.

The Birth of Jesus

In those days Caesar Augustus issued a decree that a census should be taken of the entire Roman world. ² (This was the first census that took place while Quirinius was governor of Syria.) ³ And everyone went to their own town to register.

So Joseph also went up from the town of Nazareth in Galilee to Judea, to Bethlehem the town of David, because he belonged to the house and line of David. ⁵ He went there to register with Mary, who was pledged to be married to him and was expecting a child. ⁶ While they were there, the time came for the baby to be born, ⁷ and she gave birth to her firstborn, a son. She wrapped him in cloths and placed him in a manger, because there was no guest room available for them. Luke 2:1-7 NIV

The word 'nativity' is a synonym for 'birth.' We in the Christian Church have grown to think about small wooden or ceramic figures commemorating the birth of Jesus when we hear the word 'nativity.' There has been countless art formed and/or painted around the theme of Jesus' nativity. One such beautiful art form is painted in a stained glass window at Gainesville First United Methodist Church. It is located to one's immediate left as they enter from the Narthex. Fittingly, it is first among the New Testament stories told in these beautiful windows.

We have all heard the phrase "first things first." Where we begin is so important. If we start at the wrong place, our chances increase that we will end up at the wrong place. Believing that the very Son of God began his earthly life from the womb of a young woman named Mary who was married to a compassionate carpenter named Joseph is important. To understand that the Savior of the World did not begin his earthly existence in a palace but a cattle stall is important. To comprehend that the very child of God who came to take away the sins of the world came not on a white stallion but in a cave/barn of antiquity is critical. If we can understand and comprehend such truths, then we can begin to understand God's heart for all people, even the lowest and simplest. Perhaps those who enjoy a palace find it most difficult to enjoy being saved because maybe, just maybe, they perceive they have it **all**...already.

This baby born in a home for animals and laid in a feeding trough while wrapped in swaddling clothes has been sent to this world straight from God's heart for the 'down and out' AND for the 'up and out.' Jesus has been sent to say "God loves us all." And that message is worthy of art for the centuries.

Prayer

Gracious God of new beginnings. Praise your Holy name for helping us begin in the appropriate places. Thank you for forgiving us when we get ahead of ourselves and thus ahead of you. Thank you for forgiving us when we lag behind and are afraid to start a walk of faith. Thank you for sending a baby to heal us of our brokenness and encourage us to live in good, right and fulfilling ways. Thank you for loving us so much that you gave an only child to save us from sins and our sinful selves. Gracious God of new beginnings, thank you for the babe of Bethlehem...the savior of the World. Thank you so much for so much. In the name of Jesus, Amen.

Dr. Terry Walton
Sr. Pastor
Gainesville First UMC

A Dove and Water from a Scallop-Two Symbols of Baptism

Luke 3:21-22

Now when all the people were baptized, Jesus was also baptized, and while He was praying, heaven was opened, and the Holy Spirit descended upon Him in bodily form like a dove, and a voice came out of heaven, "You are My beloved Son, in You I am well-pleased."

As soon as Jesus was baptized, he went up out of the water. At that moment heaven was opened, and he saw the Spirit of God descending like a dove and alighting on him. - Matthew 3:16

Baptism and Grace

The dove is a bird that is familiar to us throughout many stories in the Bible. In the story of Noah, a dove was the deliverer of the promise a newly created earth was forthcoming as it returned to the ark with an olive leaf in its beak. During the exile, God provided doves as food for the wandering children of Israel when they had tired of eating manna in the wilderness proving again, God would provide as promised.

In the New Testament the Holy Spirit, represented as a dove, is present in all three of Jesus' baptism accounts. Matthew and Luke tell us that immediately, as Jesus came up from the waters of baptism in the Jordan River, the heavens opened and the Spirit of God descended on him in the form of a dove and a voice from the heavens was heard saying, "This is my beloved Son, in whom I am well pleased."   John tells us that the dove descending upon Jesus identified him as one that would baptize not only with water but also with the Spirit of God. Through baptism that we are initiated into the family of God and water is the central symbol used for baptism. The liturgy used in baptism reminds us of the waters of creation and the flood, the liberation of God's people by the passage through the sea, the gift of water in the wilderness, and the passage through the Jordan River to the Promised Land. As we retell the story with each baptism, we identify ourselves with the historic people of God and join as a community with others seeking God. As the water washes over us, it symbolizes a cleansing or dying from the old life and a rising to a new life in Christ.

The scallop shell has long been recognized as a symbol of baptism and is first found in the early Western Christian church. The shell may have been part of another tradition that was adopted into the tradition as Christianity spread. Shells provided a natural bowl and small amounts of water that could be poured over the believer's head in baptism. In ancient churches there was often a shell carved into the ceiling over the altar or baptismal area signifying that this was a holy space within the church. In addition, the scallop shell has long been linked to the idea of journey or pilgrimage.

I was raised in a tradition that did not believe in baptizing infants. Older children and adults would personally make the decision that they wanted to be baptized. This approach is called "believer's baptism." As I studied the traditions of our church I came to understand that baptism is not about what "we" have done, but rather about what Christ has done. This gave me an entirely new perspective. God's generous and abundant grace is lavishly poured out for each of us. Nothing gives me greater joy than holding an infant in my arms and looking into that small face seeing the potential of that child and the promise of the family knowing that he or she will never walk alone because God promises to journey with them throughout their life.

Note:

In the United Methodist Church, Baptism and Holy Communion are the two most sacred events recognized in the life of the church. Although other denominations have more actions they consider sacred or "sacraments," the United Methodist church recognizes only Baptism and Holy Communion as sacraments because they were instituted by Christ.

Rev. Kathy Lamon

And when Jesus had been baptized, just as he came up from the water, suddenly the heavens were opened to him and he saw the Spirit of God descending like a dove and alighting on him. And a voice from heaven said, "This is my Son, the Beloved, with whom I am well pleased."

--Matthew 3:16-17

As with all of the church's holiest moments, there is in baptism something we can't quite name, an ever-elusive something that is just beyond our control. It is of God, that something; that much we know. It is a moment, and it is eternal; it is there in the words we speak, and it is beneath and beyond those words. The moment of baptism is set in motion by us and completed in and by and through God's grace.

Words are spoken, and a man is lowered into, and raised from, water, and in that simple moment is that something that is more, that is of God. The guy with the water-slicked hair is beginning anew; he is being born again, raised from the water as from death.

And on another Sunday a family brings a baby, dressed in an heirloom gown, and the people in the pews cranes their necks and ooh and ahh. Do you see that baby girl? She is a child of possibility and promise, and as water is placed on her head and words again spoken, the family that brought her and the church family that receives her claim for her an identity, a grace, a hope that includes all the generations of all the saints. There in that child's baptism is the mystery of grace spoken and shared and real before she can even understand it.

Do you feel it—that something? It is the glorious power of God's love. It is mystery and wonder.

Now, we can certainly do our best to wring the mystery and wonder right out of it all. "Preacher, we'd like to set a date to get Baby Jimmy done"—as though baptism were a vaccination. And there's that objection we Methodists sometimes hear. "What do you mean you were sprinkled? We need to get you baptized for real"—as though we can somehow control or invalidate the grace of God by the quantity of water used.

But when we take seriously this sacrament, we will experience that something beyond and beneath and within the moment, and that something is, well, really something.

John, the wild-eyed prophet, took baptism very seriously. His was a baptism of repentance. People came seeking forgiveness, a new start. Sure, some were probably caught up in the emotions of the moment. Some came simply because everyone else was coming. But far more of those people who walked into that water with John knew, or at least sensed, that something was profoundly wrong in their lives and in the world. They were looking for God.

What a scene that riverside must have been, alive with a spiritual energy, buzzing with words of power and judgment. People wept and rushed to that water, longing for forgiveness and renewal. And into that scene, that revival, came Jesus. He came to the river to be baptized by John. He came to the one who was calling people to confess their sins and repent. Why? It's a question that has given people fits for centuries. Why would the one who was without sin come to John to be baptized?

From the beginning of his gospel, Matthew has been telling us who Jesus is. Look back. There's a family tree, angelic announcements, the fulfillment of prophecies, a birth announced to magi in a distant foreign land, a star of epiphany. And now, at last, we are drawing close to the beginning of Jesus' ministry. But first, Jesus comes to John for baptism.

He is about to begin the work for which he was born. And we know what that means. We know he will spark controversy and make powerful enemies; we know his own friends will deny and abandon him and even betray him. We know about the cross. But for Jesus, standing beside the river, it is time to begin or not begin. And he has decided to begin.

Does he know fully what awaits him down that road he is about to take? I'm not sure, but he has decided that he will do what God has called him to do. He will go where he must go and do what he must do to bring people home to God. He will go where there is suffering and confusion, and he will not turn from his mission. He knows that, so he steps into the water for baptism.

All around at that river are people seeking peace with God, and awaiting him are countless others who will hear his words and look to him for forgiveness, hope, healing. But first he steps into the water. It is a moment of beginning and fulfillment. Matthew has called him *Emmanuel*, "God with us," and so now we see that truth. There in the crowd-churned mud of the Jordan River, Jesus is baptized into the fullness of human life. He enters into the reality of our world, our lives, our brokenness, and our boring days. He becomes one with us and with all people.

Do you see the widow receiving the folded flag? Jesus was baptized into that moment. The family in Monrovia, grieving and terrified as men in hazmat suits carry away their mother: Jesus was baptized into that moment. The child listening as his parents fight in the next room, the wife sitting with silent love beside her dementia-stricken husband, and you and I hobbling along with our hidden brokenness. As the waters of the Jordan sweep over him, so do all the realities of this world, all the hurts of human life, all of our regrets and longing. And should his mission with us, for us, among us, lead to the cross? So be it. He is not an angel hovering above our hurt. He has been baptized into the fullness of human life, and the fullness of human life includes death.

When Jesus steps out of the water, the Spirit, like a dove, descends, and a voice from heaven declares, "This is my Son, whom I love; with him I am well pleased." Who is Jesus? He is the one who shares complete communion with God, and he is the one who shares complete communion with us. And his power is seen in his humility. So says his baptism.

Soon—this Sunday perhaps—in your sanctuary, beneath the window with the dove descending, a family will bring their child for baptism. Such a moment is a sign of many things—repentance, new beginning, a commitment to raise the child in the faith. It is a mark of membership in the community of faith. It is a sign of God's grace. It is all these things. And it is something more, isn't it?

Behold. I will tell you a mystery. Just as Christ, in his baptism, entered into the realities of our lives, so we, in our baptism, are immersed in the fullness of Christ's life—his death, resurrection, wholeness, and love, always love.

That's something. That's really something.

Mark Westmoreland

Fayetteville First United Methodist Church

LESSONS FROM THE BOAT

In a casual observance of the Scriptures, we find that every time a boat is mentioned in the ministry of Jesus, something extraordinary is about to happen. In Matthew 8:23 – 27 we find Jesus sleeping in a boat while the disciples are worrying about the storm. Upon being awakened Jesus calms the storms and rebukes their fears! In Matt. 14:22-33 Jesus instructs the disciples to take the boat ahead of him while he prays. The disciples leave...another storm comes...and this time Jesus walks on water to them...and tells them, "Have no fear."

Jesus Calling the Disciples

Mathew 4:18-20

As Jesus was walking beside the Sea of Galilee, he saw two brothers, Simon called Peter and his brother Andrew. They were casting a net into the lake, for they were fishermen. "Come, follow me," Jesus said, "and I will send you out to fish for people." At once they left their nets and followed him.

Luke records in the fifth chapter an account of Jesus telling the distraught, fishless disciples to toss their nets on the other side and when they followed his advice their nets were completely full. Scripture says in verse eleven, "and when they brought their boats to land, they left everything and followed him." However, as the stories of the disciples unfold we find that following the death of Jesus these same enthusiastic disciples, who said they left everything and followed were found back in the same old boat, a discouraged and broken group.

These disciples had heard the call of Jesus and followed him. Now, things were different. This Jesus had been crucified. They saw him die. They heard Mary Magdalene say the Lord had risen and she had seen him (John20: 18.) They had been visited by the risen Lord and shown his hands and side (John 20:20.) He had come back a week later to give visual proof to Thomas (John 20:27.)

Now we find in John 21 the disciples had been fishing all night and had caught nothing. They heard someone talking from the beach. He told them to recast their nets on the other side. We know what happened! The fish were so great they were hard to drag into shore (scripture says 153 of them...I wonder who counted them!) The disciples knew, without a doubt, that it was the Risen Lord who had spoken to them and they then ate with him. This was the third time the disciples had witnessed the Risen Lord and from that time they never got back in their boats to fish for fish...now they fished for men!!!

When I think of these men in the boat and with Jesus as their captain there are some pretty obvious observations. In John 21 we see an example of a high and holy moment but it was a fleeting moment! Even though it was fleeting it did not take away from the fact that it happened. Do not let the down times in your life make you forget the thrill of the high moment. Examples could be legion...the joy of a birth of a new baby is not lessened when that child becomes a disobedient teenager...the excitement of getting that first job must not be forgotten when the drudgery of the daily work sets in....the thrill of falling in love and the overwhelming feeling of being love is not removed when the bills start pouring in and the money does not match the demands... the times when we, like Wesley, felt our "heart strangely warmed" must not be forgotten when our faith seems to have nothing but questions. The disciples that morning experienced a high, holy moment and they never forgot it. As we look at the boat on these beautiful windows do remember when the Lord called you out of your boat to serve him.

Also, the disciples now knew they could never get away from the Lord. They had no idea when he would again appear to them. Remember as a child you sang the song, "O be careful little eyes what you see, Oh be careful little eyes what you see. For the father up above is looking down with love. Oh be careful little eyes what you see?" There were other verses...Oh be careful little feet where you go...Oh be careful little tongue what you say. The point of the song is that Jesus is watching you and you cannot get away from his presence. As a child, these might have been words of warning but as I grow older I find that these words are words of hope, help and love. I now know, as the disciples did, they could never be far from the presence of Jesus. As you look at the window please note that the Dove, a symbol of the Holy Spirit is near the boat. The Spirit is always close to the boat of the disciples of Jesus, and that, my friends, is good news.

From that boat the disciples saw a new world. The most common occurrences reminded them of Jesus. They would eat bread and be reminded that he said, "I am the bread of life." They would walk in a room and be reminded that Jesus said, "I am the door." They would stop to pray and be reminded that Jesus said, "When you pray say…" They would see sheep and be reminded of Jesus being the Good Shepherd. These thoughts went on and on and in their lives and the strength of knowing they were living as disciples of Jesus kept them going to change the world.

In closing I leave you with one more thought. The central part of the church extending from the main door to the choir or chancel area is called the nave. The word "nave" comes from the Latin word "navis" which means ship. When we worship we sit in the boat and we hear once again the call of Christ to be His disciples and we get out of the boat and go into the world to serve. Once again as you look at these windows and see the boat and the dove, it is a call of service and a symbol of God's presence.

Dr. Phil DeMore

Senior Minister (1992-2000)

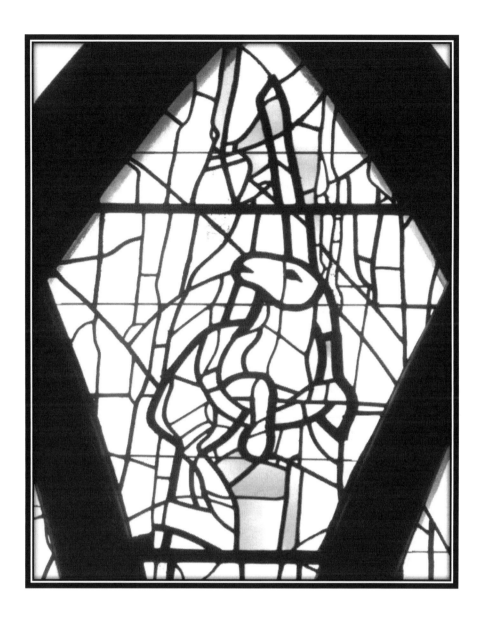

Lamb and
Shepherd's
Staff and the
Lamb

John 10:11

*I am the good shepherd.
The good shepherd lays
down his life for the
sheep.*

The Good Shepherd and the Lamb of God

One of the most common images used in Christian art or music is that of sheep. The inspiration for this is found in scripture itself. The herding of sheep, the sheep fold, the good shepherd, the sacrificial system inaugurated at God's command, all contribute to the attention we give to this element of the Biblical story. Little wonder these pastoral images are so common in churches today. David, the model king of Judah, was even described as the Shepherd King because he came from the pasture tending his sheep to the palace and tending his nation. Even Jesus used these images to convey His understanding of God's calling for His life. How do they speak to us?

They first remind us that the shepherd is one who cares for his flock.   Unfortunately, sheep seem to be ill equipped to fend for themselves.   They struggle finding food and water in that landscape that is so harsh and barren. They need help and guidance. That is just the nature of the beast.   Thus the shepherd is one who comes to guide the sheep to those places where their basic needs are met.   The good shepherd uses the crook to help guide the sheep, to pull them from the briars, protect them wild animals, and herd them into the safety of the fold.

Probably the favorite Psalm of Christendom is the 23rd Psalm.   It is recited at most funerals and in moments of distress. Consider how it begins: (KJV) 23:1 "The LORD is my shepherd; I shall not want. 2 He maketh me to lie down in green pastures: he leadeth me beside the still waters."   We need that same guidance in our lives today.   The earthly spiritual landscape is just as barren as that with which the shepherds must have contended.

In the New Testament Jesus describes His calling as a shepherd in the telling of the parable of the lost sheep. In Luke 15:3-6 (NIV) "Jesus told them this parable: 4 "Suppose one of you has a hundred sheep and loses one of them. Does he not leave the ninety-nine in the open country and go after the lost sheep until he finds it? 5 And when he finds it, he joyfully puts it on his shoulders and goes home. Then he calls his friends and neighbors together and says, 'Rejoice with me; I have found my lost sheep.'" Isn't it wonderful to think that God seeks us out personally?   You are as valuable as the rest of the flock together. Jesus, the Good Shepherd, knows you personally and will seek you out because you are so valuable to Him. John 10:11 (TEV) "I am the good shepherd, who is willing to die for the sheep." Jesus could not have been clearer in His message of love for you.   As in our window, the Good Shepherd carries us back to the fold where we enjoy safety and security.

Because the imagery of the shepherd and the sheep was familiar to His first century hearers and so compelling to those who listened,   the imagery and the explanation   of Jesus work changes from focusing on the Shepherd to the sacrifice of the lamb.   John the Baptist was the first to acknowledge this other role that Jesus fulfilled.   John 1:29-30 (NIV) records the announcement by John the Baptist, " The next day John saw Jesus coming toward him and said, "Look, the Lamb of God, who takes away the sin of the world! 30 This is the one I meant when I said, 'A man who comes after me has surpassed me because he was before me.'" The next day, John once again makes this claim about the identity of Jesus. John 1:36 (NIV) "When he saw Jesus passing by, he said, "Look, the Lamb of God!"   The Lamb of God is the one we worship. The Lamb was killed to celebrate the Passover in which the Jews put the blood of a lamb over their doorways so the angel of death would not visit their house.   The sacrifice of the Lamb would be commemorated ever year and was a high and holy day.   Later the prophet

Isaiah gave further insight to the sacrifice of the Lamb.   He prophesied   that the Lamb would carry the sins of the whole world.   Isaiah 53:4-6 (NIV) "Surely he took up our infirmities and carried our sorrows, yet we considered him stricken by God, smitten by him, and afflicted. . . 5 But he was pierced for our transgressions, he was crushed for our iniquities; the punishment that brought us peace was upon him, and by his wounds we are healed. 6 We all, like sheep, have gone astray, each of us has turned to his own way; and the LORD has laid on him the iniquity of us all."   Jesus was The Lamb of God. Nothing more nor nothing less. The prophet described him and John announced   him. Everything about our faith hinges on this reality, or else there was no reason for Christ to have sacrificed himself.

 As you stand in the sanctuary the Lamb of God is the focus of our worship.   The scriptures describe Jesus at the very center of the universe.   Indeed, today he stands at the very heart of the heavenly sanctuary and we join with the heavenly ranks in their praise.

 Revelation 5:6-13 (NIV) states "Then I saw a Lamb, looking as if it had been slain, standing in the center of the throne, encircled by the four living creatures and the elders. . . 9 And they sang a new song: "You are worthy to take the scroll and to open its seals, because you were slain, and with your blood you purchased men for God from every tribe and language and people and nation. 10 You have made them to be a kingdom and priests to serve our God, and they will reign on the earth." 11 Then I looked and heard the voice of many angels, numbering thousands upon thousands, and ten thousand times ten thousand. . . 12 In a loud voice they sang: "Worthy is the Lamb, who was slain, to receive power and wealth and wisdom and strength and honor and glory and praise!" 13 Then I heard every creature in heaven and on earth and under the earth and on the sea, and all that is in them, singing: "To him who sits on the throne and to the Lamb be praise and honor and glory and power, for ever and ever!" Amen.

Dr. Gerald Thurmond

Senior Minister (2000-2004)

The Wedding in Cana and the Miracle of Water into Wine.

John 2:1-4

And the third day there was a marriage in Cana of Galilee; and the mother of Jesus was there. And both Jesus was called, and his disciples, to the marriage. And when they wanted wine, the mother of Jesus saith unto him, They have no wine. Jesus saith unto her, Woman, what have I to do with thee? Mine hour is not yet come.

Mothers know best!

Jesus' first miracle at Canna was prompted by his mother Mary. It is as if Jesus was unsure if it was time to use his Godly powers and needed his mother to give him the go ahead.

It was a wedding I will never forget. Wedding celebrations always lasted for days as families and communities would gather to mark the occasion and to share with the newly wedded couple a wonderful beginning to marriage. The wedding was in Cana and I arrived several days early to help the family prepare for the celebration.

On the third day of the celebration, when I was helping the hostess prepare the food for the evening meal, I noticed Jesus arriving with a few men that I did not know. Just seeing him from a distance made my heart swell with love, joy and pride. I could hardly believe that more than thirty years had passed since the angel Gabriel had visited me. I remember it as if it were yesterday. Watching Jesus walk towards the wedding celebration I could still hear the angel's words:

And now, you will conceive in your womb and bear a son, and you will name him Jesus. He will be great, and will be called the Son of the Most High, and the Lord God will give to him the throne of his ancestor David. (Luke 1:31-33)

In those early days, it was difficult to believe that God had chosen me, a young, peasant girl to bare the son of the Most High. But when I first held Jesus in my arms, a peace, like I had never known filled me. At eight days old, Joseph and I took Jesus to the temple to be dedicated to the Lord. This was our custom, but it was so much more than that, it was our way of saying thank you to God. It was at the temple that we heard words of affirmation and a warning from Simeon, the priest. I have never forgotten Simeon's words as he held Jesus. Words that brought me both comfort and fear.

'This child is destined for the falling and the rising of many in Israel, and to be a sign that will be opposed so that the inner thoughts of many will be revealed—and a sword will pierce your own soul too.' (Luke 2:34-35)

These words have haunted me. I knew Jesus was sent by God and that his life would change the lives of many, but he was still my boy. The same boy who played in the sawdust of his Daddy's workshop. The same boy who we watched take his first steps and heard him speak his first word.

It was Jesus' laughter that brought me back from my memories to the wedding. He was now seated at a table surrounded by people. Jesus always was surround by people. He was a great storyteller, I imagine he must have just finished one of his stories, because everyone was laughing with him. It was a wonderful moment … music, dancing, laughter and some of the best food and wine for miles around. It was one of those moments and I tried to soak in as much as I could… to store in my heart.

Since the death of Joseph, Jesus had really become my support and companion. I treasured every conversation. My greatest joy was watching his relationship with his Heavenly Father grow and develop. His love and faith in God inspired and helped sustain me.

I knew the time was drawing near for Jesus to leave the safety of our home to begin the mission God had planned for him. I had known it was coming for some time, but a part of me wanted to hold onto him a little longer. Sometimes, my fear would get the best of me and I would cry out to God, pleading for just a little more time.

Ever since he was a small boy I had been praying that God would give me the courage to let go when it was time and the wisdom to know when that time came. That moment came while at the wedding in Cana - as I watched him talking with his friends –I realized he was no longer my little boy, but a man who was prepared and ready to be obedient to the path God had set before him.

In my heart, I knew that the time had come. It was then that I poured my soul out to God – "Grant me the courage, O Lord, to face what lies ahead. Grant me the courage, O Lord, to let him go. O Lord, help me to trust you."

As soon as I uttered those words from the depths of my heart, I heard the whispers and noticed the commotion around the headwaiter and the servants. Out of wine? How could that be?!! It would be a great dishonor to the bride and her family. Panic set in, as the headwaiter made his way over to talk with the family.

I watched as Jesus moved away from his friends to stroll out in the courtyard. I followed and spoke his name. He embraced me and asked "Are you enjoying yourself?" I nodded as I looked into his brown eyes confirming what my heart already knew. I felt torn, the mother in me wanted to protect him, to keep him close … but I knew it was time to let him go.

"Jesus", I said, "They have run out of wine." When my boy realized what I was saying he said, "I'm not ready … It's not time … not yet."

A sudden peace filled my heart. I walked away giving Jesus some time to work things out with his Heavenly Father. As I walked away, I gave my fears to God and again placed my precious firstborn into God's hands.

As I entered the house I spoke softly to the servants, "I know you need help, do whatever Jesus tells you to do." They looked at me confused, but nodded in agreement.

Several minutes later Jesus came back to the celebration and he found two servants and pointing to the 6 large, stone water jugs that had earlier been used for the ceremonial washings he said: "Fill those with water." Now they were even more confused, but they did exactly as he had instructed. Once the 6 jugs were filled with water, Jesus said, "Draw a cup and take it to the headwaiter."

The servants, not knowing what else to do, took a small cup and dipped it into one of the stone jugs and carried it to the headwaiter who quickly took a sip. His eyes lit up and for the first time all day and he smiled. He said, "Where did you get this wine?" The servants were dumbfounded but before they could respond the headwaiter turned to the groom:

"You had this magnificent wine and you saved it? At most weddings we serve the best wine first but you have saved the best for last." With a laugh, he walked away leaving a stunned and surprised groom behind him. The headwaiter instructed the servants to serve the wine to the guests. Disaster had been avoided – the family had been saved from disgrace and the wedding celebration continued.

In that moment I remembered the final words the angel spoke to me long ago:

"Nothing will be impossible with God."

Jesus performed his first miracle, a sign of what was to come. My heart swelled once again with joy, love and pride. Jesus surprised even me. He took ordinary water and transformed it into wine, not just any wine, but really good wine. And not just a little wine, but an extravagant amount of wine.

The men surrounding Jesus were amazed at what he had done and they began to ask him questions and to believe the things the he said to them.
I smiled … knowing that this was an indication of greater things to come. Jesus would be the one who would bring joy and abundant life to all people. Jesus would be the one who would meet every human need with the provision, power and love of God.

My eyes once again sought out the eyes of my boy. I now realized that my job as the mother of Jesus was finished. Jesus' ministry had begun. He no longer belonged to me, but to his Heavenly Father.

And I once again whispered to the Lord, just as I had done more than thirty years ago, "Here I am, a servant of the Lord."

Rev. Wendy Cordova

T

Matthew 9:20-22 (Mark 5:25-34; Luke 8:43-48)

And suddenly, a woman who had a flow of blood for twelve years came from behind and touched the hem of His garment. For she said to herself, "If only I may touch His garment, I shall be made well." But, Jesus turned around, and when He saw her He said, "Be of good cheer, daughter; your faith has made you well." And the woman was made well from that hour.

That this story appears in three of the four Gospels would suggest that its message is most important. The mention of twelve years confirms the seriousness of the sickness and thus the difficulty of curing it. It appears the woman's problem was a menstrual disorder, perhaps a light flow

96

Mark 5: 24-29

And a certain woman, which had an issue of blood twelve years, And had suffered many things of many physicians, and had spent all that she had, and was nothing bettered, but rather grew worse, When she had heard of Jesus, came in the press behind, and touched his garment. For she said, If I may touch but his clothes, I shall be whole. And straightway the fountain of her blood was dried up; and she felt in her body that she was healed of that plague.

throughout the month. Leviticus 15: 25-26 indicates that such a condition made the woman and everything she touched ritually unclean. Hence she would have been isolated from society-a lonely, helpless outcast. Yet, this woman fought her way desperately through the crowd in order to touch Jesus. As soon as she did so, she was healed. What a contrast between the crowds that were curious about Jesus and the few who reach out and touch Him. Many people are familiar with who Jesus is, but nothing in their lives is changed by knowing He is God's son. It is only faith in Christ that releases God's healing power. Are you just curious about God, or do you reach out to him in faith, knowing that His mercy will bring healing to your body, soul, and spirit?

This miracle is an example of faith in Jesus by someone in an impossible and dire situation. The woman touched Jesus' cloak and was healed without him purposefully doing anything. It was not until after the fact that he felt something had left him and that the woman kneeled at his feet did he realizes what had happened. He said to her,

"Daughter, your faith has healed you. Go in peace and be freed from your suffering."

Rev. Richard Pletsch

Leviticus 15:25

"If a woman has a discharge of blood many days, but not at the time of her monthly period, or has a discharge that continues beyond the time of her period, she is unclean."

Those words, from our Law Book summarized my life from the time I was age 13 until the day I touched Him. More about Him later but before that part of my story, you need to know how my life was impacted by the menstrual cycle that begin for me, like most other girls at around my age, but unlike all of my friends, my period never ended. I was a healthy Jewish girl with loving parents, who although poor, were committed to living by the standards set out from our father Moses hundreds of years earlier. That commitment meant regular Sabbath worship including the sacrifice of pigeons and doves purchased from the money changers, which unlike the wealthier worshipers, was all that my father could afford. So it was with great trepidation that my father, who loved me so much, felt that he should report my condition to the leader of our local synagogue, Jairus. Perhaps because a baby daughter had just been born to Jairus, or he and my father were friends, Jairus tried to keep my condition quiet, his only instruction to my parents was that until I stopped "bleeding", I could not accompany them into the Synagogue. Not only was this of traumatic embarrassment to me, but it broke my father's heart, especially when one of the other religious officials, a leading Pharisee, felt it his duty to declare my condition in public. On a sunny day as I walked with my mother in the market place, he shouted the words from the book of Leviticus for everyone to hear.

My life was never the same after that. No boys saw me as an appropriate candidate for marriage. As an unmarried adult daughter, I became a financial burden to my family since could only work at certain task to help supplement our family income. My primary job was as a helper to non-Jewish man who tanned and sold animal hides. Since this was also a "unclean" profession under our law, not only was I allowed to work in his shop, but the smell of the hides help mask the odor of my body, which was impossible to control even with daily bathing. When there was money available, and that was rare, I would spend it with traveling healers and doctors. They readily took the money but never delivered on their promises of healing.

It was during one hot day in the shop when I first heard about Him. Oh I had already heard of the healing of the blind and lame and other miracles He was performing. Some of our Synagogue leaders said He was a fake, but this did not deter the desperate sick along with just the curious from forming huge crowds where ever He went. I knew that the daughter of Jairus, now a young teenager, had been sick. I did not know that he had summoned the carpenter's son to come to his house to heal her until the street in front of the shop became congested with people. As I went to the door, I not only saw Him for the first time, but was compelled by a sudden sense of urgency to get to Him. Perhaps if I could just touch Him, for some strange reason I was sure He would heal me. This time, my 'unclean 'status was an advantage to me, as those who recognized me, moved aside. Still I had to push my way through the crowd and just as I was within reach I stumbled and fell. Everything seemed to go into slow motion; the noise of the crowed went almost silent, like voices in a distance. Without looking up I did it. My fingertips barely touched the helm of His garment, but the sensation of cleansing was euphoric and immediate. I knew that my physical condition had been completely healed, but without understanding how or why, a cleansing of my soul had also occurred. My plan now was to quietly slip away. But then He stopped walking and turned back to my direction. When He asked who had touched Him I was still on my knees. The crowed grew silent again and with my face bowed and my body trembling; I told Him it was me. What He said next changed my life forever. "Daughter, your faith has made you well; go in peace and be healed of your affliction." He turned and started back in the direction of Jairus' home.

Years later, that daughter of Jairus, now an adult, and I would talk about the day both our lives were change by His touch. We became good friends and she and I both had children of our own. We were crushed when we heard that our Healer had been crucified. But then some of His followers began to tell of a resurrection and an empty tomb. As usual, many doubted, especially the religious leaders, those same theologians who had condemned me to a life of uncleanness and discounted the healing of Jairus' daughter as trickery or demon involvement. But she and I knew better, because nothing could be more real than what had happened to each of us. Reportedly, a Roman Centurion in charge of His execution had exclaimed that He was indeed the Son of God. We knew that truth some two years earlier. Plus, His presence remained with us the rest of our lives.

Homer Myers

Why a Boat?

All of us who grew up hearing of Jesus teaching from a boat, particularly Mark 3: 5-9 and forward through chapter 4 in its entirety, know the parable of the sower so well that we hardly focus on the words we hear. And we seldom, if ever, consider the boat from which the words were spoken as anything of importance. Yet, as I turned to the chapter today and began to read, I noted the significance of the parable as related to where the message was spoken – and why.

As a child I delighted in a familiar tale about the fisherman and his wife in which the husband goes to the water to plead with the fish, saying, "Fish of the Sea, Come listen to me – my wife Isabel has a wish to tell." The

Jesus Preaches from Boat

Mark 3:5-9

Jesus withdrew with his disciples to the lake, and a large crowd from Galilee followed. When they heard about all he was doing, many people came to him from Judea, Jerusalem, Idumea, and the regions across the Jordan and around Tyre and Sidon. Because of the crowd he told his disciples to have a small boat ready for him, to keep the people from crowding him.

husband then expresses his wife's wish to this "fish of the sea" and expects a response.

This childhood fairy tale well describes the "multitude" from whom Jesus sought to remove himself and his disciples to a "place apart," a boat off shore from those who pressed around him and swelled into a crowd. Such a crowd might easily be recognized in the swarm of riotous clamor around many of today's music icons or other celebrities, crowds seeking to "touch" them or hail them with avid reaching for something of their person, a piece of cloth or a relic from which some "miracle" might occur. The crowd on shore, too, expects miracles from Jesus, wishing him to act as a king or a savior, some who are sick and wish for healing, others with wishes for him to serve as a protector.

But Jesus seems to have something else in mind. And he wants his disciples to know it. So, he goes off shore, in sight and "hearing" of the crowd, but with a more or less private session with his chosen few, the disciples themselves. To the crowd, he does deliver parables, which, at this point in his ministry, seems to be an attempt to have them receive the message rather than focusing on him as a person of "celebrity." He realizes that within this focus on his person, the "message" of his ministry has become lost, has not been "heard." By distancing himself in a boat, he takes the focus off himself and offers the message. He says in verse 9 of this fourth chapter of Mark that he wants those who "hath ears to hear" to get the "message," not merely the words that, like the seeds, have "fallen on fallow ground" as his parable details.

Jesus speaks also of the seeds which "fall by the wayside" and are devoured by (in symbolic form) the winds of chance; some "falling on stony ground" and having no depth, a symbolic surface hearing which withers when the sun comes up and the "heat is on," so to speak. This last reference seems to be itself a prophecy of sorts, because Jesus knows that his ministry is going well at this time, but the time is coming when these multitudes will be tested in their devotion and will abandon his message because the words he has spoken to them here on this day have been absorbed on the surface only and have not developed roots to sustain the rays of the sun when the going gets rough. He speaks of other "seeds" falling among thorns, and the acceptance of the words becoming choked by surrounding obstacles in the form of a crowd mentality caught up in the latest group psyche. Still other seeds "fall on good ground and yield fruit that [sprang] up and increased."

Alone, in the boat Jesus explains that this "good ground" is about to be further "separated from the crowd" when he takes his twelve and interprets the parables to them – in Mark 4:10, they are said to "ask him of the parable" and he relates that it has been a message to the people *about* his ministry itself. In Mark 4: 11-20, he takes each portion and makes specific references to each part. Here, we can see clearly that it is *in the boat* that he delivers the explanation of the parable, his "message" being delivered to the disciples themselves. Although usually read from pulpits and in ministers' sermons today as if the explanations of the parables were spoken to the crowd, it is to the disciples alone with him on the boat that he speaks the words *they* are to hear. Verse 14 reads, "without a parable, he spake not the word unto them, as they were able to *hear* it." Again, he is speaking to the disciples, not to the multitude.

Significantly, Jesus at this point suggests to the disciples, "Let us pass over unto the other side." I wonder that the disciples did not question this notion of getting "unto the other side." Did not any of them question Jesus? And, if they did not, what did they "expect" to be the outcome of this journey to the other side? It is at this time that there arises a "great storm of wind, and the waves beat into the ship...." Then, the disciples rush to him, admonishing him (much as the fairy tale fisherman admonished the fish of the sea to "come listen to me"). Here now, they ask the most basic question of all, one that arises most naturally and one which Jesus already anticipated. "Master, carest thou not that we perish?" Immediately, he rebukes the wind with, "Peace, be still."

Most climactic of all the scriptures on faith seems to reach an apex here on the boat at this very crucial point as Jesus turns to his disciples and poses his own query to *them*, "Why are ye so fearful? How is it that ye have no faith?" These are the disciples themselves, those closest to him, not the crowd they've left, but those "few" to whom he has just delineated every aspect of the spreading of the word through the sower parable, but who have quite obviously neither heard nor heeded the words of the parable of the sower in regard to the "seeds taking root." When the wind rises and the boat founders, they lose their base at once.

We aren't finished yet, for what is probably the most powerful verse (41) comes, not from Jesus and his preaching on the boat, but from the disciples themselves here on the boat with him who raise a question among themselves from the midst of the open sea, "What manner of man is this, that even the wind and sea obey him?" Here, now, on the boat, the seeds of the message begin bringing forth fruit in the sense of this emerging (sprouting) of the seeds of faith.   They have recognized the message.

So it is that the boat itself has offered the opportunity for those "who have ears to hear" to grasp the message, a message St. Paul later set forth when he admonished us all to "Keep the Faith," to open ourselves to the hearing which means more than just hearing, but requires continued action and commitment to standing faithful when the "crowds" around thin out and you are left "alone in the boat."

Janice K. Watts

Jesus Ascended and Crowned as King

Mark 16:19

So then after the Lord

had spoken unto them,

he was received up into

heaven, and sat on the

right hand of God.

Willet Stained Glass Studio's Interpretation of Jesus Ascension Window

"Through the central part of the window is a circle representing the world from which He ascended to sit in glory crowned as King, on a throne from which flows the river of the water of life between the trees of life."

Leaving To Be More Fully Present

The Ascension is perhaps one of the least understood, least emphasized and most marginalized portions of the Christian story. Yes, it is a part of the Apostle's Creed: "ascended into heaven and sitteth at the right hand of the Father". But does this mean that Jesus has left us? Does He now sit on some far off throne in power and majesty removed from us, waiting to return at some uncertain future while we wait in the lurch? These questions point to the lack of appreciation for the deeper meaning of and importance of the Ascension to our faith journey. Such remoteness is the very opposite of what the ascension really means to us. In reality, it was a story of connection, of empowerment, of commissioning God's people for the work of the Gospel, not one of disconnection and loss of power. It was the experience and witness of the early church that Jesus in his ascension became more present, more available to all who trust and lean on Him. How is this? Jesus in his early life was available only to those in close contact with Him. After his death and resurrection, He again appeared to his disciples, but these appearances were limited in time and place. However, in his ascension, just as He had promised, He would be present for all people, at all times through the presence of the Holy Spirit. Hence the Ascension is really a deep and powerful affirmation of the real presence of Christ for all people, at all times.

The stained glass windows illustrate this understanding with imagination and clarity, as the ascending Jesus has his feet still resting firmly in the world that He loves so much. And He touches the tree of life with both of his hands. He has left us, but is even more connected to all. This ongoing sense of connectedness and empowerment is not just in the imagination of the artist who created these panels. It is firmly grounded in the Biblical story. All of the Gospels speak of the commissioning and empowering of the followers of Jesus after his resurrection.

The writing of Luke is even more explicit about the Ascension. Luke 24:49 tells us that the resurrected Jesus came to his disciples and reminded them: *"And see, I am sending upon you what my Father promised; so stay here in the city until you have been clothed with power from on high."* Luke 24:50-51 tells of the Ascension: *"Then he led them out as far as Bethany, and lifting up his hands, he blessed them. While he was blessing them, he withdrew from them and was carried up into heaven. "* This story of the ascension is so important to Luke that when he writes his 2nd volume, which we call Acts, he told the story again adding a few more details. In Acts 1, the disciples are in Jerusalem waiting and praying just as they had been instructed and Jesus appears to them and says: *"But you will receive power when the Holy Spirit has come upon you* (which takes place in Acts 2)*; and you will be my witnesses in Jerusalem, in all Judea and Samaria, and to the ends of the earth. When he had said this, as they were watching, he was lifted up, and a cloud took him out of their sight. While he was going up and they were gazing up toward heaven, suddenly two men in white robes stood by them. They said, "Men of Galilee, why do you stand looking up toward heaven? This Jesus, who has been taken up from you into heaven will come in the same way as you saw him go into heaven."* In other words, He will come again, but in the meantime, don't just stand around. There is work to be done-Kingdom work. And we are not alone in this work. Jesus promised to and did indeed send His Spirit, the Holy Spirit, His presence and power to be with us as we do the work of the Gospel during the "meantime".

The victory of Easter has not ended, the dynamic power of the Incarnation is still with us. We are not alone. Through the ascension of Jesus, we now have the presence and power of Jesus with us at all times, in all places, through the Holy Spirit. Thus, we are empowered to live as Kingdom people. Thanks be to God!

Dr. John Cromartie

John 19: 29

A jar of wine vinegar was there, so they soaked a sponge in it, put the sponge on a stalk of the hyssop plant, and lifted it to Jesus' lips.

John 19: 36-37

These things happened so that the scripture would be fulfilled: "Not one of his bones will be broken, and as another scripture says, "They will look on the one they have pierced."

Mark 15:20

And when they had mocked him, they took off the purple robe and put his own clothes on him. Then they led him out to crucify him.

Ps 22:18

"They part my garments among them, and cast lots upon my vesture."

The Cloth of the Mocking Cross

A different type of cross adorns our sanctuary during the time preceding Easter. The wood of the cross is rough and the design simple. What makes this cross, The Mocking Cross, different from other times of the year is the purple cloth that is draped over the cross beam (Lat. *patabulum*). Iconographer Charles Z. Lawrence of Willet Stained Glass Studios also included other accoutrements of the cross. There is the crown of thorns and crossed at its base is a spear and a sponge each attached to a pole. One might wonder why a rooster, a flagrum, a reed, a nail, a hammer, and the superscription (Lat. *titulus*) which Pilate inscribed "Jesus the Nazarene-The King of the Jews" were not depicted as well. Each of these items has their own important role in the Passion (Lat. *suffering*) of Jesus. However, because it is the material that adorns the patabulum that makes this cross different from other times of the year, the focus here will be on the cloth. The cloths of The Passion mentioned in the scripture are intricately woven throughout the fabric of the journey of Jesus to the cross.

The Passion of Jesus is that time encompassed by the arrest, trial, suffering and ends with his crucifixion. Caiaphas, the high priest of Jerusalem and President of the Sanhedrin, had Jesus arrested in the garden of Gethsemane (Lat. *olive press*) shortly after the Last Supper. He was first taken to Annas (John 18:12-14), the father in law of Caiaphas who was a previous high priest. Setting the tone throughout the several trials over the next many hours Jesus speaks little and doesn't attempt to defend himself. He is beaten, mocked and then sent back to Caiaphas. Of note, it is during the interrogation of Jesus by Annas that Peter denies Jesus three times in the palace courtyard. (John 18:15-27) Hence, the rooster also is often depicted as an accoutrement of the cross.

It is now night time and the Sanhedrin is not in session, so Caiaphas questions Jesus and imprisons him in his palace in anticipation of the trial planned for the next morning, April 15, 30 A.D., by the Sanhedrin. The Sanhedrin finds Jesus guilty of blasphemy for claiming to be "The Son of God." Because this body of Jewish leaders can condemn but cannot execute someone, Jesus is sent to the Roman governor of Judaea, Pontius Pilate. The Sanhedrin's hope is that by morphing the charge of blasphemy into the concept of Jesus being "King of the Jews" they will entice Pilate to crucify Jesus on the basis of sedition (threatening the sovereignty of Emperor Tiberius), which was a Roman charge punishable by death. During this trial Pontius learns that Jesus is a Galilean and as such is under the jurisdiction of the tetrarch Herod Antipas (whose claim to fame was that of serving the head of John the Baptist to his wife on a silver platter). Pilate promptly forwards Jesus on to Herod who happened to be in Jerusalem at the time and was only a short distance away. (Luke 23:7)

Herod Antipas whose father Herod the Great, who had attempted to kill the baby Jesus 30 years before, was more interested in preserving his relationship with the Sanhedrin and possibly being entertained by Jesus performing miracles than in conducting a trial. Jesus again refuses to answer questions or defend himself, and the mocking and beating that had become a part of the ritual since the arrest continues. It is here that the soldiers of Herod place on Jesus a "gorgeous robe" that is meant to mock him as well as ridicule the title referring to Him as King of the Jews. (Luke 23:11) One notes that the meeting with Herod is only mentioned in Luke and that there is no mention of the color of the robe. Is this the cloth that is draped over the Mocking Cross?

Herod, serving no purpose in this affair other than continuing the beatings and mockery of Jesus sends him back to Pilate. The political consequences of putting Jesus to death by crucifixion was something not lost on Pilate. He knows Rome expects him to keep the Jews in check without disruptions or uprisings and condemning an innocent man, a popular one at that, was something he'd prefer to avoid.

After brief questioning and getting nothing back from Jesus but clever replies, the ever-evasive Pilate, having misgauged the ultimate intent of the Sanhedrin, attempts to free Jesus by using a custom that allows him to release a prisoner before Passover. Yet again the crowd assembled is influenced by the Chief Priests of the Sanhedrin who are among them. They choose to crucify Jesus and release Barabbas, the murderer and thief, instead. (Mark 15:11)

Pilate then hopes to appease the Sanhedrin by ruthlessly scourging Jesus (repeated lashes to the back while attached to an iron ring with hands tied), ruthlessly thereby avoiding having to decree that Jesus be put to death. The instrument for the scourging is the flagrum which has three leather thongs, each bearing metal balls and bone, the purpose of which is to tear the flesh. Although at this point the formal pronouncement that Jesus be put to death by crucifixion has not been made, the Roman ritual "preparing one for crucifixion" has begun in earnest as Jesus is now severely dehydrated, weakened by beatings, and losing bodily fluids through open wounds on his neck, back and legs as a result of the scourging. The scourging of Jesus is done in Pilate's palace Praetorium where a twisted crown of thorns is placed on His head, he is given a reed meant to symbolize a king's staff, and adorned with a robe. All these combined actions proceed from an effort to mock Jesus as "The King of the Jews." Of note, this robe has been described both as scarlet (Matthew 27:28) and purple (John 19:2). Whether it was a red shade of purple or a purple shade of red, again Jesus is mocked through a robe color suggesting royalty. It has been supposed that the "gorgeous robe" that Herod placed on Jesus earlier in the day may very well have been the same one used here. After the flogging, Jesus is taken from The Praetorium (which was felt to be unclean for the Jews), and brought out into The

Pavement, the open space in which Pilate's judging seat was located and where it was acceptable for the Jews to congregate.

If Pilate thought that beating Jesus again by scourging would suffice in deterring the Sanhedrin's wish for crucifixion, he was mistaken. Of the crowd of Jews that had assembled to witness this trial, members of the Sanhedrin were inculcated. Knowing full well the consequence and threat to their power by Jesus having overturned the money changers' tables at the Temple, it was imperative to them that he die. Passover the next day gave immediacy to this desire. Pontius washes his hands in front of the crowd and says, "I am innocent of this man's blood. It is your responsibility." (Matthew 27:24) Jesus is then led away to be crucified. Again there is a reference to cloths of the passion as, before they lead Jesus away, they remove the robe and put his clothes back on. (Matthew 27:31) The robe placed over Jesus' scourged body in addition to the healing mechanisms of the body had probably begun to seal the flesh wounds and stem further loss blood and fluids. Removing the robe would have reopened these wounds and worsening his dehydrated state. This weakened physical condition caused by scourging is what the Roman crucifixion death squad hoped to achieve in all of its condemned men before crucifixion-- increase the suffering and yet hasten the time to death on the cross.

The distance from The Praetorium to Golgotha is about .3 miles and, although Jesus is depicted carrying an entire cross, the condemned usually were given only the crossbeam to carry. The crossbeam weighed about 75 pounds. Simon of Cyrene, who had come to Jerusalem for the Passover from Cyrene, Libya, was compelled by the Romans to help Jesus carry the crossbeam. Although not mentioned in the Gospels, along the way a woman named Veronica offers a piece of cloth to wipe the sweat from Jesus' forehead. This cloth later becomes the Veil of Veronica and Veronica's kindness is represented in the Catholic Church as the sixth station of the cross.

Once the upright portion of the cross (the stipe) was reached beyond the outer walls of the city, Jesus again was stripped and thrown on his back in order to attach him to the crossbeam. This was achieved with nails that were 5-7 inches in length and a diameter of 3/8 of an inch at the head. Contrary to what has been believed, the nails were most likely placed between the two bones of the forearm as opposed to the hands. The crossbeam and Jesus were then lifted and attached to the stipe. Additional nails were placed in the feet with the legs bent to accommodate placing one foot over the other. A seat (sedulum) was sometimes placed on the stipe to prolong the time to death, but in Jesus' case, with Passover approaching, the Roman guards needing a quick death and most probably did not use this or the foot rest (suppendaneum). Each of these additions to the cross helped the condemned by enabling the torso and feet to improve respiration and thus delay the death, usually caused by hypovolemia and asphyxiation. At this time, the description of the crime (previously written by Pontius) is attached to the top of the cross.

The crucifixion detail was not the most desirable of duties for the Roman soldiers and as an incentive to their unpleasant job they were allowed to keep any possessions or garments of the person crucified. Jesus had on a tunic, an undergarment which had been made in a seamless fashion by his mother. Because of this type construction the guards were unable to divide it into parts so they cast lots for Jesus' tunic. (John 19:23-24) The material of the tunic would have been of a common material and there is no mention in the Gospels of it being purple or having color. That lots would be cast for Jesus' tunic was foretold in Psalm 22:18.

By Roman law a concoction of vinegar wine and myrrh was offered to Jesus on two occasions. The myrrh was added as an analgesic. The first time Jesus declined the liquid (Mark 23:15) was because he preferred to remain conscious and experience his suffering with a clear mind. He did accept it the second time after stating, "I thirst."(John 19:28) This also fulfilled the scripture as stated in Psalm 69:21. The wine vinegar was offered to him on a sponge attached to hyssop. (John 19:29-30) One recalls that Moses instructed the Jews to apply the blood of a lamb with a hyssop plant on the lintel of the door during the Passover in Egypt. Just as the blood of the sacrificial lamb saved the Israelites in Egypt, so too Jesus as the sacrificial lamb is given up for the sins of others.

One of the duties of the Roman death squad was to stay with the condemned until they were certain the crucified was dead. Often times the legs would be broken with a large mallet to hurry the process. The broken bones of the legs not only caused internal bleeding but more importantly negated the use of legs in supporting the body and facilitate breathing and thus hastening death. The Jewish elders wanted the bodies off the cross because of the coming of Passover. The Roman guard did break the legs the criminals on either side of Jesus, but upon reaching Jesus, they noted he was already dead. To prove that Jesus was dead, he was speared on his right side by the Roman guard. Water and blood emanated forth and the soldier was content that Jesus was dead. (John 19 32-34) This also fulfilled the scripture that, "He protects his bones, not one of them will be broken." (Psalm 34:20) Hence, the crossed spear and sponge were included in the symbol of the cross.

Joseph of Arimathea, a member of the Sanhedrin, boldly obtained permission from Pilate to take Jesus down from the cross for a proper burial. In doing so he took risks in alienating himself as member of the Sanhedrin and because touching a corpse violated Jewish law. He bought fine linen in which to wrap Jesus in for placement in a tomb hewn in rock which he possessed. (Mark 15:46)

One can imagine the process of taking a lifeless, limp, grown man whom you love down from a cross to which he is attached by nails under the downward pressure of gravity. Nicodemus and Joseph, who only hours ago were present at the assembled Sanhedrin in which Jesus was condemned, using a ladder placed sheets of cloth under Jesus' arms and waist to support the dead weight of his body while the nails were driven in the reverse direction to free the body from the cross. The release of the body was done in a sequential fashion as the support of the nails having been removed gave way to the supporting cloth. When all the nails had been driven out, Jesus then was slowly lowered, using the cloth, into the arms of Joseph, as His mother Mary watched. As Jesus descended there was a mighty earthquake. The fine linens brought by Joseph were used to wrap Jesus with the 75 lbs of aloe and myrrh provided by Nicodemus in preparation for the sepulchre (tomb). As it was the day of preparation for Jewish Passover a tomb nearby and not previously used was chosen for Jesus. (John 19:42) Does the cloth of the cross represent the linens used to facilitate taking Jesus down from the cross?

Mary Magdalene on the first day of the week goes to the tomb to find the stone moved and Jesus gone. Simon Peter and John run to the tomb with John beating Peter there, however he only looks in; he doesn't go into the tomb. Peter gets there, and, in keeping with his impetuous character, goes immediately into the tomb. Here he sees the burial linens, but something else is specifically mentioned. The face cloth is rolled and separate from the other cloths. (John 20:6-7) The significance of this detail is debated, but all agree that the cloth being rolled and not just thrown about shows that the disappearance of Jesus was not rushed or hurried as one would expect if his body had been stolen. It implies that He left in an orderly fashion and of a time of His choosing.

So The Mocking Cross in our church begins The Passion with purple linen draping its crossbeam and ends Easter with a white one signifying both the trial and the triumph of Jesus. All of the symbols in our windows chosen by Rev. Thompson tell an important story but none more so than the cross and its accoutrements.

Now about that face cloth, or handkerchief, or napkin in which Jesus' head was bound but then found so nicely rolled and put aside. It is of interest that some relate the head cloth to a custom whereby if the master leaves the table with his napkin folded that the servants are not to clean the table because this indicates the master will be coming back.

You can almost hear Rev. Thompson saying after quite reflection, "Tonight after you've cleared the table and done the dishes... you might want to make sure your house is in order too."

John McHugh

The Phoenix

Job 29:18-20

Then I said, I shall die in my nest, and I shall multiply my days as the sand. My root was spread out by the waters, and the dew lay all night upon my branch. My glory was fresh in me, and my bow was renewed in my hand.

The mythical Phoenix is said to have built a nest, set it on fire and then to have risen from the ashes in victory. The Phoenix has become symbolic of the resurrection, immortality and the life-after-death of Jesus.

Dr. Thompson referred to this figure as a "kite." A kite was one of the birds that the Jews were forbidden to eat. Dr. Thompson felt the figure looked too much like the dove in the window depicting baptism and not a Phoenix. This is one of many things he wanted improved or changed but Henry Willet's health deteriorated and as such nothing was done. If you look at the Phoenix and then at the dove in the baptism window you'll note that they do look similar.

Myth of the Phoenix and the Christian Tradition

Myth is a narrative attempt to explain the unexplainable, usually depicting heroic characters performing supernatural deeds. Evolving through centuries of oral tradition, myths often embellish historical facts with imaginative, fantastic details, providing a rich basis for many religious traditions and practices. Such myth surrounds the elusive, magical bird known as the Phoenix.

The legendary Phoenix originated in Egyptian mythology as a bird which periodically consumed itself in flames and subsequently rose anew out of its own ashes. Its image synthesizes the appearance and characteristics of two actual birds-the pheasant and the eagle. Symbolically the pheasant is associated with family and fertility, whereas the eagle traditionally represents freedom and strength.

Although the mystical Phoenix was a widespread, popular myth throughout the ancient world, the earliest reference found in Christian orthodoxy is attributed to Roman Catholic Church Father, Pope Clement I of Rome. In writing to the early church at Corinth, Clement directly stated, "there is a bird called the Phoenix," drawing on the legend's familiarity and popularity among early Christians. Moreover, Clement implies the symbolic parallel between Christ's resurrection and the bird's rebirth out of his own ashes. A further detail specified by Clement in the expanding Phoenix mix is that the bird's nest was of "frankincense and myrrh," spices traditionally associated with the Magi gifts at Christ's birth.

Additional details linking the pagan mythological bird with Christian traditions continued in the centuries following Pope Clement I. One such detail was the bird's returning to life after three days, paralleling Christ's three days of death before the resurrection. Fourth and fifth century Church Fathers like Ambrose, Cyril, and Jerome continued to repeat the myth of the Phoenix, even offering it as God's proof in the natural world of the reality of Christ's resurrection.

James Ewing

The Last Supper

(Rev. Patricia Southerland's Last Supper is included with the Passover window.)

Matthew 26:17-25

On the first day of the Festival of Unleavened Bread, the disciples came to Jesus and asked, "Where do you want us to make preparations for you to eat the Passover?"

He replied, "Go into the city to a certain man and tell him, 'The Teacher says: My appointed time is near. I am going to celebrate the Passover with my disciples at your house.'" So the disciples did as Jesus had directed them and prepared the Passover.

When evening came, Jesus was reclining at the table with the Twelve. And while they were eating, he said, "Truly I tell you, one of you will betray me."

They were very sad and began to say to him one after the other, "Surely you don't mean me, Lord?"

Jesus replied, "The one who has dipped his hand into the bowl with me will betray me. The Son of Man will go just as it is written about him. But woe to that man who betrays the Son of Man! It would be better for him if he had not been born."

Then Judas, the one who would betray him, said, "Surely you don't mean me, Rabbi?"

Jesus answered, "You have said so."

The windows of the First United Methodist Church were truly a collaborative effort. Charles Lawrence designed the windows for The Willet Stained Glass Studios of Philadelphia, Pa. based on subject matter from The Old and New Testament chosen by Reverend Jim Thompson. The principle of the Willet Studios, Henry Willet, who was in his eighties when this project began, constructed the windows. Ingrid Barker, the daughter of James Barker of Barker and Cunningham Architects, also provided valuable input using her degree in Iconoclastic Interior Design to integrate the windows into the plans for the sanctuary.

THE NARTHEX

THE STORY OF THE ONGOING CHURCH

Pentecost

Acts 2:1-4

Now when the day of Pentecost had come, they were all together in one place. Suddenly a sound like a violent wind blowing came from heaven and filled the entire house where they were sitting. And tongues spreading out like a fire appeared to them and came to rest on each one of them. All of them were filled with the Holy Spirit, and they began to speak in other languages as the Spirit enabled them.

Ten days after Jesus ascended into heaven, the twelve apostles, Jesus' mother and family, and many other of His disciples gathered together in Jerusalem for the Jewish harvest festival that was celebrated on the fiftieth day after Passover. While they were indoors praying, a sound like that of a rushing wind filled the house and tongues of fire descended and rested over each of their heads. This was the outpouring of the Holy Spirit on human flesh promised by God through the prophet Joel.

(Joel 2:28)

"And afterward, I will pour out my Spirit on all people. Your sons and daughters will prophesy, your old men will dream dreams, your young men will see visions."

Pentecost. Wind and Fire.

The Pentecost window depicts the moment when the power of God descends on the waiting disciples and empowers them to change the world in the name of the risen Christ. The story in Acts 2:1-21 is also the story of the birth of the church. Christians who enter our church under the picture of the disciples, set afire by the tongues of flame atop their heads, enter to encounter the Spirit in a place where we gather to be renewed, to listen and understand the call of Christ, and to hear and share stories of "God's deeds of power" in scripture, in our own individual lives and in the lives of Christians everywhere. We enter as a scattered people, busy with our own lives, with our own troubles, with our own priorities. We enter, often weighed down by the cares and chaos of our everyday world.   Just as the disciples gathered among people "from every nation under heaven", we gather from all directions and all manner of coming and going. And we come to be renewed by the Spirit, and to be challenged, like the first disciples, to listen to the words of the prophets and the teachers, and to "...see visions," and to "...dream dreams." And then, empowered by the living Spirit of Christ, equipped to speak the languages of the world into which we travel, we go out into the byways and highways of our lives, to make disciples for Christ for the transformation of the world.

Dr. Richard Puckett

p

Henry Willet's report on the Windows:

"Peter on the roof top seated with the symbolic animals in his lap is great and I feel is in perfect character and harmony with our first Christian martyr Stephen on the other side. I don't see how you can improve that."

Although the figure above certainly looks like a man on his back and consistent with Stephen being stoned as the first martyr, it actually represents Paul being thrown from a horse on the road to Damascus and representing his conversion to Christianity. The top arch windows represent figures of the ongoing church and for that reason it makes sense to represent Paul and Peter on either side of the Pentecost window. If you closely you'll see a horse looking down at Paul. Paul being thrown by a horse is not mentioned in the bible, however much like the horns that are given to Moses because of Michelangelo's Sculpture of Moses depicting horns, a famous painting The *Conversion on the Way to Damascus*, a masterpiece by Caravaggio painted in 1601 for the Cerasi Chapel of the church of Santa Maria del Popolo, in Rome has helped perpetuate that interpretation of scripture.

Acts 9:1-19

120

Paul's Conversion

Saul is in a hurry. Armed with letters from the high priest in Jerusalem to the synagogues in Damascus, he is breathing threats and murder against the disciples of the Lord, and he is on his way to arrest followers of the Way. As Saul approaches Damascus, suddenly there is a bright light from heaven and he hears a voice, "Saul, Saul, why do you persecute me?" He falls to the ground and asks, "Who are you, Lord?" the reply came, "I am Jesus, whom you are persecuting. Get up and enter the city and you will be told what to do." Saul blinded by the light, is led into Damascus by his companions. This is a dramatic story of Paul's conversion from Saul, chief persecutor to the early Christians to Paul, chief missionary and theologian of the Early Church. In the city a man named Ananias is called by the Lord to restore Paul's sight and to give him god's mission: "He is an instrument whom I have chosen to bring my name before Gentiles and kings and before the people of Israel." Ananias does as the Lord commands, and Paul is baptized and begins to proclaim the Jesus is the Messiah in the synagogues of Damascus.

Paul's conversion is the key event in his life of faith. He tells the story of this life changing experience three times in the Book of Acts: the first account is in Acts 9; the second in Acts 22 as he is arrested in Jerusalem by a Roman tribune; and the third is in Acts 26 as Paul stands as a prisoner in Caesarea before the King Agrippa. Throughout Paul's letters to the churches he has founded, he calls himself an Apostle, because the Risen Christ appeared to him on the road to Damascus.

Paul's conversion experience and subsequent ministry to the Gentiles and Jews in Corinth and Ephesus and Galatia and Philippi and across the Mediterranean has raised a question for Christians down through the centuries: Is it necessary to have a Damascus Road experience like Paul's in order to become a Christian? Many church members have heard powerful testimonies of sinful lives transformed by a confession of belief in Christ, and they sometimes feel that if they haven't had an earth shattering conversion they aren't really Christians. Certainly Christ still calls us, "Come follow me"; yet he call us by name, individually, in our unique human circumstance. Some persons experience a dramatic conversion like Paul's; others come to the Christ through gradual growth and commitment in their own hearts.

John Wesley, the founder of Methodism, was an eighteenth century Anglican priest who had been a missionary to Georgia, but he was still unsure of his salvation. Then on May 24, 1738, he attended a meeting on Aldersgate Street in London. Someone read from Luther's Preface to the Epistle to the Romans. Wesley later wrote, "While he was describing the change which God works in the heart through faith in Christ, I felt my heart strangely warmed. I felt I did trust in Christ, Christ alone for salvation; and an assurance was given me that He had taken away my sins, even mine, and saved me from the law of sin and death." From that day on John Wesley became an inspired preacher who spread the message of God's grace across England for over fifty years.

Paul Tillich, the renowned twentieth century theologian, wrote a sermon titled "You Are Accepted", which gives a quieter description of conversion and the human experience of sin and grace. He wrote that when we feel stuck in a meaningless and empty life, full of despair which destroys joy and courage, something happens: "At that moment a wave of light breaks into our darkness, and it is as though a voice were saying: 'You are accepted. *You are accepted*, accepted by that which is greater than you, and the name of which you do not know. Do not ask for the name now; perhaps you will find it later. Do not try to do anything now; perhaps later you will do much. Do not seek for anything; do not perform anything; do not intend anything. *Simply accept the fact that you are accepted!'* If that happens to us, we experience grace. After such an experience, we may not be better than before, and we may not believe more than before. But everything is transformed. In that moment, grace conquers sin, and reconciliation bridges the gulf of estrangement." As a college freshman at Northwestern University, I read these words of Tillich for the first time in a Methodist Student foundation small discipleship group. They changed my life. I felt God's love and acceptance in a powerful way, and that assurance of grace has led me on my journey of faith for fifty years.

Paul's conversion on the road to Damascus, depicted in this stained glass window, is a sign-post for the Christian life. Every Christian has a story to tell of one's experience of grace. In I Peter 3:15, we find these words: "Always be ready to make your defense to anyone who demands from you an accounting for the hope that is in you." You are called by God, called by name. Always be ready to tell the story of how God in Christ has transformed your life through love and grace. Tell the old, old story of Jesus and his love!

Rev. Ferris Hendley Hardin

Peter's Rooftop Vision

Acts 10:9-13

About noon the following day as they were on their journey and approaching the city, Peter went up on the roof to pray. He became hungry and wanted something to eat, and while the meal was being prepared, he fell into a trance. He saw heaven opened and something like a large sheet being let down to earth by its four corners. It contained all kinds of four-footed animals, as well as reptiles and birds. Then a voice told him, "Get up, Peter. Kill and eat."

The two principal characters in the book of Acts, which describes many episodes in the life of the early Christian Church, are Peter and Paul.

Above Peter is shown experiencing a landmark vision. While sleeping on a rooftop he had a vision of a variety of animals let down from heaven on a sheet which he is commanded to eat. He refuses since they are not kosher and the reply comes "What God hath cleansed that call not common." Almost immediately after comes a call from a centurion Cornelius whom Peter welcomes into the Church as the first Gentile Christian.

Peter's Rooftop Vision

Initially it may seem puzzling that a window representing Peter's strange vision occupies the prominent space over the front entrance of our church. With so many beautiful images from which to choose, why this? Some background on the book of Acts puts this vision in context and helps to explain its significance.

Acts (Acts of the Apostles) continues the narrative of Luke's Gospel and traces the story of the Christian movement from the crucifixion and resurrection of Jesus to the time when the apostle Paul was in Rome preaching the gospel unhindered. Most of the first half of Acts is occupied with the Jerusalem church in which Peter takes a leadership role. The Disciples in Jerusalem boldly speak God's word, teach and heal and thousands of "believers" – from Jerusalem and nearby villages - receive the gift of the Holy Spirit and are baptized. Though the message is beginning to spread, the Disciples did not consider themselves starting a new church. They were Jews. They went to the Temple and followed Jewish customs. Their message was for Jews. Their desire – as was Jesus' - was to reform Judaism and to bring to it a new dimension.

Peter's Rooftop Vision enters here as an integral part of the story of Cornelius, a Roman centurion, who becomes the first Gentile Christian. Cornelius and his household were God-worshippers who gave generously to those in need and prayed to God constantly. He is visited by an angel who instructs him to send messengers to Joppa where Peter is staying to summon him to Cornelius' home. God is taking the initiative and Cornelius responds. At the same time, God is aware that Peter will need extra encouragement to move him out of his Jewish comfort zone, so he sends Peter a vision of a large sheet descending from heaven containing all kinds of animals, reptiles and birds, which he is told to kill and eat. As a faithful Jew, Peter cannot conceive of eating common or unclean meat, and yet the vision appears 3 times, leaving Peter bewildered by its meaning; however it is again God's taking the initiative to bring Peter and the Gentiles together by communicating with him both visually and audibly. The sheet from heaven and the voice bear witness to Peter that all God's creatures are to be viewed as clean and good, not to be refused. To fulfill God's purpose, Peter's must also share Israel's blessings with the Gentiles.

Cornelius' servants arrive with the invitation for Peter to join Cornelius at his home in Caesarea, saying that this request was dictated by a holy angel. Not only can Peter not imagine eating common animals, neither can he imagine entering the home or accepting the hospitality of a meal with a Gentile. He is torn between custom and conviction. Throughout the text, Peter is slowly beginning to shake ethnic prejudices that were ingrained in him. The Holy Spirit is at work, whittling away at Peter's heart as he approaches those he has been taught to avoid.

Entering Cornelius' home, Peter reminds him that it is unlawful for him, a Jew, to associate with or to visit with a Gentile, but says "God has shown me that I should not call anyone profane or unclean." Peter understands and declares the truth of his vision that "God shows no partiality; whoever worships him and does what is right is acceptable to him." Peter now knows that Jesus is Lord of all. He preaches the word of Jesus, tongues are spoken, and Gentiles are baptized. Peter, as well as Cornelius and perhaps more dramatically, was baptized to new life as inclusivity begins to replace his prejudice.

It is easy, safe and comfortable to hold abstract truths about inclusiveness and justice when we don't have to face the challenge of practicing those truths where we live and work. Might our judgment of others be limited by the short-sightedness of our own vision rather than by the depth and breadth of God's vision?

Peter's Rooftop Vision can remind us to open our minds and reverse the conventional categories of who is in or who is out. God's love is to be available to all. God's spirit is moving around us in unexpected and challenging ways. What better image to appear above our door! We believe it is no accident that Dr. Jim Thompson, working with the designers of the windows, wanted to convey that Gainesville First United Methodist would be a church of "open hearts, open minds and open doors", many years before this was officially adopted by the United Methodist Church. May we always strive to make this so.

Lynda Askew and Sally Darden

St. Augustine of Hippo's Seal

354-430 A.D.

A flaming heart transfixed by an arrow in gold is of the human heart transfixed by Divine Love. This is the traditional emblem of St. Augustine of Hippo depicting his famous quotation from Confessions, *Chapter 1: "Our hearts shall ever restless be, until they find their rest in Thee."*

Augustine of Hippo was born in Tagaste on the northern coast of Africa, now Souk-Ahras, Algeria. His father, Patricius Aurelius, saw his brilliant potential and provided him an excellent education in Tagaste and later in Carthage. Augustine, against his father's wishes, then returned to Tagaste to teach "grammar." He had to find his way through various enticing philosophical errors and heresies of that period. His rebuttals of them opened up pathways for the Christian faith ever since.

The age-old questions regarding God and His creation were what occupied his mind. God, the eternal one, all good, created the universe and human beings. These He created good and endowed them with intelligence and freedom. Whence evil? Did God create it? Did it always exist? Did God will it to exist? Since God knows everything and especially the eventual outcome of His creating action, is He really the ultimate source of evil, especially of moral evil? Does His foreknowledge mean that everything is predestined and cannot be otherwise? Do we really have a free will?

Mani (216? - 276?) from Persia taught that there were two eternal sources, one of good and the other of evil. Rebutting this, Augustine said all works of God are good and moral evil is due to the misuse of the liberty of intelligent creatures, not God, who foresaw this misuse and went ahead with His act of creation.

The Donatists, from the 2nd century, were very concerned over the holiness of the Church. Specifically, could a sinner be pardoned and remain in the bosom of the Church? Do the ministerial powers of a bishop or his ordained helpers depend on their moral worthiness? Augustine's position was that the ordained ministers are God's instruments and He is not impeded by their moral unworthiness. Then too the Church can tolerate sinners within its pale for the sake of converting them.

Pelagius (390-418) attacked the doctrine of original sin, i.e. the consequences for the human family: death, concupiscence, murder, and a whole list of evil actions. Augustine: humans were not created in that condition. Pelagius claimed that that was the condition in which Adam and Eve were created and therefore there was no fallen condition that we inherited. No "sin" that we inherit.

Arius (250-336) started the heresy that bears his name. He denied the Triune nature of God, and that Jesus had two natures, human and divine. Hence He was born into the same condition as we all have. Because He was such a righteous person, God called Jesus His son. He, in turn, referred to God as His father. Arius' teachings were heresy and Augustine wrote and preached against them. Eventually at the Council of Nicea, 325 AD, the heresy was condemned, and Arius exiled.

Augustine's writings were voluminous and influenced the direction of the Church's preaching and teaching even down to our times. He still serves us in subordinating reason to authority in the teachings of the Church. Theologians still mine his writings to get a better grasp of Christian teachings.

Monsignor Bill Hoffman

Martin Luther's Seal

1483-1546 A.D.

A heart with a black cross superimposed on it on as stylized rose.

Few men have impacted, not only church history, but world history like Martin Luther. His words, his faith, and his passion moved princes, popes, and paupers. Martin Luther and the reformation sparked from his life are memorialized in the left panel of the narthex. There you will find the Seal of Martin Luther, which is also called the Luther Rose. The seal contains five components. It begins with a black cross inside a red heart. The heart is surrounded by a white rose that lies upon a field of sky blue. Completing the seal is a golden ring around the seal.

The Seal of Martin Luther encapsulates the doctrine he championed called "justification by faith alone." This belief holds that it is not actions in the church, works of any kind, or any task performed that brings salvation into a person's life. It is by faith in Jesus Christ that we are saved. Luther is credited with the development of this doctrine; although, he would be quick to point to the Apostle Paul, other biblical texts, and Saint Augustine as proponents of this doctrine.

Let us turn to the seal and see how the imagery teaches justification by faith alone. Martin Luther himself describes the meaning of his seal in a letter he penned to Lazarus Spengler, July 8, 1530. Lazarus Spengler sent a drawing of the seal to Luther wanting to know if Luther approved. In Luther's response, he expresses his delight in the seal and explains how the seal is a summary of his theology.

The black cross in a red heart together serve as a reminder that it is through faith in Jesus Christ, who was crucified, that saves from sin. Even though the cross is black and should "hurt," the cross does not "kill but keeps [man] alive." (Luther 359) The heart is the spring from which life giving faith arises.

The white rose is a symbol of the fruits of salvation. Luther names these fruits as joy, comfort, and peace. He then states there is a fundamental difference between the peace and joy of the world and the true peace and true joy from faith. They are wholly separate. The peace and joy from faith being much greater. To show this difference, the rose in the seal is white instead of red.

The sky blue field symbolizes that we have a future heavenly hope of a greater joy and peace. The peace and joy found on earth in this life through salvation is just a foretaste of the greater manifestation of peace and joy to come.

Finally, the golden ring encircling the sky blue field is a description of the ultimate heavenly joy and peace that awaits the faithful. The preciousness of the peace and joy of heaven surpasses all others just as gold surpasses the preciousness of all other metals. The golden ring is a circle without end. This is to speak to the truth that heaven is an everlasting blessing, also without end.

Martin Luther's impact may not have occurred if it were not for a chance, or not so chance, rain storm. Luther was a promising young law student, which was a profession his father Hans wanted him to pursue. Luther was traveling on the road near the village of Stotternheim. A violent rain came. Luther feared for his very life. In that moment of fear Luther cried out, "Help, St. Anne, I will become a Monk." (Marius 43) Luther survived the storm and although, many tried to talk him out of his vow because of his promise as a law student, Luther kept his word. He became a monk in the Augustinian order in the city of Erfurt.

Luther was a faithful monk. He was ordained to the priesthood in 1507. In 1508, the recently founded University of Wittenberg was in need of teachers. The dean of theology, Johann von Staupiz was also an Augustinian monk. He sent word of his need for teachers to the Augustinians in Erfurt. They sent him Luther. Luther taught a variety of subjects in philosophy and theology before settling in as the Doctor of Bible at the University, receiving his bachelors and doctor degrees in the process.

It was while studying the bible at Wittenberg that the doctrine of justification by faith became his prominent theme. Luther began teaching this doctrine for several years at Wittenberg without incident. In fact in the university, the message was being accepted by many. It was the outworking of this belief that sparked the conflict.

At this time in Rome, Pope Leo X required money to finish St. Peter's basilica. Luther's archbishop Albrecht of Brandenburg also needed money to pay off his debts garnered to acquire his appointments. This led to an agreement between Leo X and Albrecht to sell papal indulgences in Albrecht's territory. They would split the profits. Indulgences are connected to the sacrament of penance that brings a person back into the communion of faith following some sin. Indulgences do not always involve money, but the ones that caught Luther's eye did.

Luther, believing that forgiveness and restoration come by faith alone, saw the sale of indulgences as a works based system. It upset him to see the hard working people of Wittenberg spending their money in such a way. Like any good monk, he wrote a letter to Archbishop Albrecht on October 31, 1517. In this letter, he outlined topics for debate that centered around the sale of indulgences and if the practice is biblical. This letter is known as the 95 Theses.

There are several factors that allowed this simple act of sending a letter to his archbishop to become a reformation that engulfed Europe for centuries. First, the demand of money upon German Catholics from Rome was a burden, and one they resented. Second, Luther's writings took full advantage of the relatively new technology of the printing press. The 95 Theses was printed and disseminated quickly. It was all over Germany in weeks and Europe in months. This happened to Luther's other writings as well. Lastly, Luther used crass and sometimes downright vulgar language. This style of writing made him a sensation because monks and priests just didn't use that kind of language. The people ate it up.

Luther found fast supporters. Frederick of Saxony who ruled Wittenberg protected Luther. The people of Germany rallied behind him making an arrest of Luther by the Catholic Church a difficult task. Luther continued to write pamphlets and engaged in debate in an attempt to reform the Catholic Church, not break from it; but neither side was willing to budge.

At the Diet of Augsburg (October 1518), Luther debated Cardinal Cajetan on the authority of the Pope, who supported the sell of indulgences. The Cardinal asked Luther to recant. Luther refused. Luther was sneaked out of the city at night for his safety. Later, Luther faced John Eck in public disputation in early 1519. Eck was skilled in the art of debate. He maneuvered Luther into agreeing with some points of the theology of John Huss which were similar to justification by faith. Huss was already condemned as a heretic. This admission to an already condemned heresy gave the Catholic Church the grounds to act against Luther.

Luther continued to write against current practices of the Catholic Church. He was a prolific writer. At this time, he wrote in support of justification by faith. He wrote against the Catholic Church's seven sacraments saying that only two (baptism and communion) come from the bible. He wrote that if the church wouldn't reform itself, German nobility should step in and force reforms.

With the continued writings against long held beliefs and the confession of agreement with a condemned heretic, the Catholic Church issued a papal bull in 1520 that would excommunicate Martin

Luther unless he recanted within 60 days. Luther, faced with the difficult decision of life under excommunication or recant, held a public burning of the papal bull on June 15, 1520.

Shortly after his excommunication, Luther was given safe conduct by Charles V to attend the Diet of Worms in April of 1518. Luther hoped to have a debate on his books and ideas, but the powers that be just wanted to know if he would recant. Disappointed that productive discussion was not possible, Luther responded by saying, "my conscience is captive to the Word of God. I cannot and I will not recant anything, for to go against conscience is neither right nor safe. God help me. Amen." (Marius 294) Fearing that Luther would be killed for his stand in Worms, Frederick arranged for Luther to be kidnapped and taken to the castle of Wartburg for his own protection.

While at the Wartburg, Luther struggled with depression, temptation, and demons but soon returned to writing. He wrote against monastic vows, private confession being compulsory, and other topics. Without question, his most significant contribution at this time was to translate the New Testament into German, giving the bible to the common people for the first time.

Luther eventually left the Wartburg to take the reins of his movement. He travelled, preached, and continued to write. He helped free monks and nuns who could not choose to leave the monastic lifestyle. He ended up marrying an escaped nun named Katharina von Bora with whom he had six children. Luther helped organize the Lutheran Church writing much of their doctrine, polity, and catechisms. He worked and served right up until the end preaching his last sermon just three days before his death on February 18, 1546.

Luther was far from perfect. Going through battle after battle, he eventually equated his enemies with the devil. His pen became a mighty weapon. His crass and vulgar language that made him an entertaining read, at times crossed lines. He put down his enemies so harshly in ink that his views led to bigotry and worse to those that crossed him. The Peasants' Rebellion and his views on the Jews are just two examples.

With his flaws, Luther was a man who empowered individuals to build a personal relationship with God. To summarize Luther, I believe one should say that above all he wanted individuals to have the power to live a life of faith. Luther never wanted to eradicate the church. Quite the opposite is true. He wanted the church to be a source of encouragement to the people, not a burden. His teaching of justification by faith taught that you can reach God without priest or rite. His rejection of five sacraments was to lift the dependence on church ritual off the people so they could have more access to God. He gave license for monks and nuns to turn from their vows if they chose. They could make their own choice on how to follow God. He translated the bible into German. For the first time the common man could read the very word of God. Luther wanted to empower individuals to commune with God; he wanted a church to support this empowerment. He surely had the fire to stand and to fight for this empowerment against an institution.

For further reading

Owen Chadwick, *The Penguin History of the Church 3: The Reformation.* New York, NY: Penguin Books, 1972 p. 11-75

Martin Luther, *Luther's Works: Volume 49.* Edited and translated by Gottfried G Krodel, and edited by Helmut T. Lehmann. Philadelphia, PA: Fortress Press, 1972 p. 356-359

Richard Marius, *Martin Luther: The Christian Between God and Death.* Cambridge, MA: The Belknap Press of Harvard University Press, 1999

Dr. Jesse Colbert

In May 1738, clergyman John Wesley attended a meeting of Moravians in Aldersgate Street. While attending the meeting, he underwent a profound religious experience, describing it in his journal thus:

"In the evening I went unwillingly to a society in Aldersgate Street, where one was reading Luther's preface to the Epistle to the Romans. About a quarter to nine, while he was describing the change which God works in the heart through faith in Christ, I felt my heart strangely warmed. I felt I did trust in Christ, Christ alone for salvation, and an assurance was given me that he had taken away my sins, even mine and saved me from the law of sin and death."

This moment was for Wesley an awakening to the assurance found in salvation by grace alone and has been referred to by scholars as a defining moment in the Methodist movement.

Preface to the Letter of St. Paul to the Romans

by Martin Luther, 1483-1546

Translated by Bro. Andrew Thornton, OSB

This letter is truly the most important piece in the New Testament. It is purest Gospel. It is well worth a Christian's while not only to memorize it word for word but also to occupy himself with it daily, as though it were the daily bread of the soul. It is impossible to read or to meditate on this letter too much or too well. The more one deals with it, the more precious it becomes and the better it tastes. Therefore I want to carry out my service and, with this preface, provide an introduction to the letter, insofar as God gives me the ability, so that every one can gain the fullest possible understanding of it. Up to now it has been darkened by glosses [explanatory notes and comments which accompany a text] and by many a useless comment, but it is in itself a bright light, almost bright enough to illumine the entire Scripture.

To begin with, we have to become familiar with the vocabulary of the letter and know what St. Paul means by the words law, sin, grace, faith, justice, flesh, spirit, etc. Otherwise there is no use in reading it.

You must not understand the word law here in human fashion, i.e., a regulation about what sort of works must be done or must not be done. That's the way it is with human laws: you satisfy the demands of the law with works, whether your heart is in it or not. God judges what is in the depths of the heart. Therefore his law also makes demands on the depths of the heart and doesn't let the heart rest content in works; rather it punishes as hypocrisy and lies all works

133

done apart from the depths of the heart. All human beings are called liars (Psalm 116), since none of them keeps or can keep God's law from the depths of the heart. Everyone finds inside himself an aversion to good and a craving for evil. Where there is no free desire for good, there the heart has not set itself on God's law. There also sin is surely to be found and the deserved wrath of God, whether a lot of good works and an honorable life appear outwardly or not.

Therefore in chapter 2, St. Paul adds that the Jews are all sinners and says that only the doers of the law are justified in the sight of God. What he is saying is that no one is a doer of the law by works. On the contrary, he says to them, "You teach that one should not commit adultery, and you commit adultery. You judge another in a certain matter and condemn yourselves in that same matter, because you do the very same thing that you judged in another." It is as if he were saying, "Outwardly you live quite properly in the works of the law and judge those who do not live the same way; you know how to teach everybody. You see the speck in another's eye but do not notice the beam in your own."

Outwardly you keep the law with works out of fear of punishment or love of gain. Likewise you do everything without free desire and love of the law; you act out of aversion and force. You'd rather act otherwise if the law didn't exist. It follows, then, that you, in the depths of your heart, are an enemy of the law. What do you mean, therefore, by teaching another not to steal, when you, in the depths of your heart, are a thief and would be one outwardly too, if you dared. (Of course, outward work doesn't last long with such hypocrites.) So then, you teach others but not yourself; you don't even know what you are teaching. You've never understood the law rightly. Furthermore, the law increases sin, as St. Paul says in chapter 5. That is because a person becomes more and more an enemy of the law the more it demands of him what he can't possibly do.

In chapter 7, St. Paul says, "The law is spiritual." What does that mean? If the law were physical, then it could be satisfied by works, but since it is spiritual, no one can satisfy it unless everything he does springs from the depths of the heart. But no one can give such a heart except the Spirit of God, who makes the person be like the law, so that he actually conceives a heartfelt longing for the law and henceforward does everything, not through fear or coercion, but from a free heart. Such a law is spiritual since it can only be loved and fulfilled by such a heart and such a spirit. If the Spirit is not in the heart, then there remain sin, aversion and enmity against the law, which in itself is good, just and holy.

You must get used to the idea that it is one thing to do the works of the law and quite another to fulfill it. The works of the law are every thing that a person does or can do of his own free will and by his own powers to obey the law. But because in doing such works the heart abhors the law and yet is forced to obey it, the works are a total loss and are completely useless. That is what St. Paul means in chapter 3 when he says, "No human being is justified before God through the works of the law." From this you can see that the schoolmasters [i.e., the scholastic theologians] and sophists are seducers when they teach that you can prepare yourself for grace by means of works. How can anybody prepare himself for good by means of works if he does no good work except with aversion and constraint in his heart? How can such a work please God, if it proceeds from an averse and unwilling heart?

But to fulfill the law means to do its work eagerly, lovingly and freely, without the constraint of the law; it means to live well and in a manner pleasing to God, as though there were no law or punishment. It is the Holy Spirit, however, who puts such eagerness of unconstained love into the heart, as Paul says in chapter 5. But the Spirit is given only in, with, and through faith in Jesus Christ, as Paul says in his introduction. So, too, faith comes only through the word of God, the Gospel, that preaches Christ: how he is both Son of God and man, how he died and rose for our sake. Paul says all this in chapters 3, 4 and 10.

That is why faith alone makes someone just and fulfills the law; faith it is that brings the Holy Spirit through the merits of Christ. The Spirit, in turn, renders the heart glad and free, as the law demands. Then good works proceed from faith itself. That is what Paul means in chapter 3 when, after he has thrown out the works of the law, he sounds as though the wants to abolish the law by faith. No, he says, we uphold the law through faith, i.e. we fulfill it through faith.

Sin in the Scriptures means not only external works of the body but also all those movements within us which bestir themselves and move us to do the external works, namely, the depth of the heart with all its powers. Therefore the word *do* should refer to a person's completely falling into sin. No external work of sin happens, after all, unless a person commits himself to it completely, body and soul. In particular, the Scriptures see into the heart, to the root and main source of all sin: unbelief in the depth of the heart. Thus, even as faith alone makes just and brings the Spirit and the desire to do good external works, so it is only unbelief which sins and exalts the flesh and brings desire to do evil external works. That's what happened to Adam and Eve in Paradise (cf. Genesis 3).

That is why only unbelief is called sin by Christ, as he says in John, chapter 16, "The Spirit will punish the world because of sin, because it does not believe in me." Furthermore, before good or bad works happen, which are the good or bad fruits of the heart, there has to be present in the heart either faith or unbelief, the root, sap and chief power of all sin. That is why, in the Scriptures, unbelief is called the head of the serpent and of the ancient dragon which the offspring of the woman, i.e. Christ, must crush, as was promised to Adam (cf. Genesis 3). *Grace* and *gift* differ in that grace actually denotes God's kindness or favor which he has toward us and by which he is disposed to pour Christ and the Spirit with his gifts into us, as becomes clear from chapter 5, where Paul says, "Grace and gift are in Christ, etc." The gifts and the Spirit increase daily in us, yet they are not complete, since evil desires and sins remain in us which war against the Spirit, as Paul says in chapter 7, and in Galations, chapter 5. And Genesis, chapter 3, proclaims the enmity between the offspring of the woman and that of the serpent. But grace does do this much: that we are accounted completely just before God. God's grace is not divided into bits and pieces, as are the gifts, but grace takes us up completely into God's favor for the sake of Christ, our intercessor and mediator, so that the gifts may begin their work in us.

In this way, then, you should understand chapter 7, where St. Paul portrays himself as still a sinner, while in chapter 8 he says that, because of the incomplete gifts and because of the Spirit, there is nothing damnable in those who are in Christ. Because our flesh has not been killed, we are still sinners, but because we believe in Christ and have the beginnings of the Spirit, God so shows us his favor and mercy, that he neither notices nor judges such sins. Rather he deals with us according to our belief in Christ until sin is killed.

Faith is not that human illusion and dream that some people think it is. When they hear and talk a lot about faith and yet see that no moral improvement and no good works result from it, they fall into error and say, "Faith is not enough. You must do works if you want to be virtuous and get to heaven." The result is that, when they hear the Gospel, they stumble and make for themselves with their own powers a concept in their hearts which says, "I believe." This concept they hold to be true faith. But since it is a human fabrication and thought and not an experience of the heart, it accomplishes nothing, and there follows no improvement.

Faith is a work of God in us, which changes us and brings us to birth anew from God (cf. John 1). It kills the old Adam, makes us completely different people in heart, mind, senses, and all our powers, and brings the Holy Spirit with it. What a living, creative, active powerful thing is faith! It is impossible that faith ever stop doing good. Faith doesn't ask whether good works are to be done, but, before it is asked, it has done them. It is always active. Whoever doesn't do such works is without faith; he gropes and searches about him for faith and good works but doesn't know what faith or good works are. Even so, he chatters on with a great many words about faith and good works.

Faith is a living, unshakeable confidence in God's grace; it is so certain, that someone would die a thousand times for it. This kind of trust in and knowledge of God's grace makes a person joyful, confident, and happy with regard to God and all creatures. This is what the Holy Spirit does by faith. Through faith, a person will do good to everyone without coercion, willingly and happily; he will serve everyone, suffer everything for the love and praise of God, who has shown him such grace. It is as impossible to separate works from faith as burning and shining from fire. Therefore be on guard against your own false ideas and against the chatterers who think they are clever enough to make judgements about faith and good works but who are in reality the biggest fools. Ask God to work faith in you; otherwise you will remain eternally without faith, no matter what you try to do or fabricate.

Now *justice* is just such a faith. It is called God's justice or that justice which is valid in God's sight, because it is God who gives it and reckons it as justice for the sake of Christ our Mediator. It influences a person to give to everyone what he owes him. Through faith a person becomes sinless and eager for God's commands. Thus he gives God the honor due him and pays him what he owes him. He serves people willingly with the means available to him. In this way he pays everyone his due. Neither nature nor free will nor our own powers can bring about such a justice, for even as no one can give himself faith, so too he cannot remove unbelief. How can he then take away even the smallest sin? Therefore everything which takes place outside faith or in unbelief is lie, hypocrisy and sin (Romans 14), no matter how smoothly it may seem to go.

You must not understand flesh here as denoting only unchastity or spirit as denoting only the inner heart. Here St. Paul calls flesh (as does Christ in John 3) everything born of flesh, i.e. the whole human being with body and soul, reason and senses, since everything in him tends toward the flesh. That is why you should know enough to call that person "fleshly" who, without grace, fabricates, teaches and chatters about high spiritual matters. You can learn the same thing from Galatians, chapter 5, where St. Paul calls heresy and hatred works of the flesh. And in Romans, chapter 8, he says that, through the flesh, the law is weakened. He says this, not of unchastity, but of all sins, most of all of unbelief, which is the most spiritual of vices.

On the other hand, you should know enough to call that person "spiritual" who is occupied with the most outward of works as was Christ, when he washed the feet of the disciples, and Peter, when he steered his boat and fished. So then, a person is "flesh" who, inwardly and outwardly, lives only to do those things which are of use to the flesh and to temporal existence. A person is "spirit" who, inwardly and outwardly, lives only to do those things which are of use to the spirit and to the life to come.

Unless you understand these words in this way, you will never understand either this letter of St. Paul or any book of the Scriptures. Be on guard, therefore against any teacher who uses these words differently, no matter who he be, whether Jerome, Augustine, Ambrose, Origen or anyone else as great as or greater than they. Now let us turn to the letter itself.

The first duty of a preacher of the Gospel is, through his revealing of the law and of sin, to rebuke and to turn into sin everything in life that does not have the Spirit and faith in Christ as its base. [Here and elsewhere in Luther's preface, as indeed in Romans itself, it is not clear whether "spirit" has the meaning "Holy Spirit" or "spiritual person," as Luther has previously defined it.] Thereby he will lead people to a recognition of their miserable condition, and thus they will become humble and yearn for help. This is what St Paul does. He begins in chapter 1 by rebuking the gross sins and unbelief which are in plain view, as were (and still are) the sins of the pagans, who live without God's grace. He says that, through the Gospel, God is revealing his wrath from heaven upon all mankind because of the godless and unjust lives they live. For, although they know and recognize day by day that there is a God, yet human nature in itself, without grace, is so evil that it neither thanks nor honors God. This nature blinds itself and continually falls into wickedness, even going so far as to commit idolatry and other horrible sins and vices. It is unashamed of itself and leaves such things unpunished in others.

In chapter 2, St. Paul extends his rebuke to those who appear outwardly pious or who sin secretly. Such were the Jews, and such are all hypocrites still, who live virtuous lives but without eagerness and love; in their heart they are enemies of God's law and like to judge other people. That's the way with hypocrites: they think that they are pure but are actually full of greed, hate, pride and all sorts of filth (cf. Matthew 23). These are they who despise God's goodness and, by their hardness of heart, heap wrath upon themselves. Thus Paul explains the law rightly when he lets no one remain without sin but proclaims the wrath of God to all who want to live virtuously by nature or by free will. He makes them out to be no better than public sinners; he says they are hard of heart and unrepentant.

In chapter 3, Paul lumps both secret and public sinners together: the one, he says, is like the other; all are sinners in the sight of God. Besides, the Jews had God's word, even though many did not believe in it. But still God's truth and faith in him are not thereby rendered useless. St. Paul introduces, as an aside, the saying from Psalm 51, that God remains true to his words. Then he returns to his topic and proves from Scripture that they are all sinners and that no one becomes just through the works of the law but that God gave the law only so that sin might be perceived.

Next St. Paul teaches the right way to be virtuous and to be saved; he says that they are all sinners, unable to glory in God. They must, however, be justified through faith in Christ, who has merited this for us by his blood and has become for us a mercy seat [cf. Exodus 25:17, Leviticus 16:14ff, and John 2:2] in the presence of God, who forgives us all our previous sins. In so doing, God proves that it is his justice alone, which he gives through faith, that helps us, the justice which was at the appointed time revealed through the Gospel and, previous to that, was witnessed to by the Law and the Prophets. Therefore the law is set up by faith, but the works of the law, along with the glory taken in them, are knocked down by faith. [As with the term "spirit," the word "law" seems to have for Luther, and for St. Paul, two meanings. Sometimes it means "regulation about what must be done or not done," as in the third paragraph of this preface; sometimes it means "the Torah," as in the previous sentence. And sometimes it seems to have both meanings, as in what follows.]

In chapters 1 to 3, St. Paul has revealed sin for what it is and has taught the way of faith which leads to justice. Now in chapter 4 he deals with some objections and criticisms. He takes up first the one that people raise who, on hearing that faith make just without works, say, "What? Shouldn't we do any good works?" Here St. Paul holds up Abraham as an example. He says, "What did Abraham accomplish with his good works? Were they all good for nothing and useless?" He concludes that Abraham was made righteous apart from all his works by faith alone. Even before the "work" of his circumcision, Scripture praises him as being just on account of faith alone (cf. Genesis 15). Now if the work of his circumcision did nothing to make him just, a work that God had commanded him to do and hence a work of obedience, then surely no other good work can do anything to make a person just. Even as Abraham's circumcision was an outward sign with which he proved his justice based on faith, so too all good works are only outward signs which flow from faith and are the fruits of faith; they prove that the person is already inwardly just in the sight of God.

St. Paul verifies his teaching on faith in chapter 3 with a powerful example from Scripture. He calls as witness David, who says in Psalm 32 that a person becomes just without works but doesn't remain without works once he has become just. Then Paul extends this example and applies it against all other works of the law. He concludes that the Jews cannot be Abraham's heirs just because of their blood relationship to him and still less because of the works of the law. Rather, they have to inherit Abrahams's faith if they want to be his real heirs, since it was prior to the Law of Moses and the law of circumcision that Abraham became just through faith and was called a father of all believers. St. Paul adds that the law brings about more wrath than grace, because no one obeys it with love and eagerness. More disgrace than grace come from the works of the law. Therefore faith alone can obtain the grace promised to Abraham. Examples like these are written for our sake, that we also should have faith.

In chapter 5, St. Paul comes to the fruits and works of faith, namely: joy, peace, love for God and for all people; in addition: assurance, steadfastness, confidence, courage, and hope in sorrow and suffering. All of these follow where faith is genuine, because of the overflowing good will that God has shown in Christ: he had him die for us before we could ask him for it, yes, even while we were still his enemies. Thus we have established that faith, without any good works, makes just. It does not follow from that, however, that we should not do good works; rather it means that morally upright works do not remain lacking. About such works the "works-holy" people know nothing; they invent for themselves their own works in which are neither peace nor joy nor assurance nor love nor hope nor steadfastness nor any kind of genuine Christian works or faith.

Next St. Paul makes a digression, a pleasant little side-trip, and relates where both sin and justice, death and life come from. He opposes these two: Adam and Christ. What he wants to say is that Christ, a second Adam, had to come in order to make us heirs of his justice through a new spiritual birth in faith, just as the old Adam made us heirs of sin through the old fleshy birth.

St. Paul proves, by this reasoning, that a person cannot help himself by his works to get from sin to justice any more than he can prevent his own physical birth. St. Paul also proves that the divine law, which should have been well-suited, if anything was, for helping people to obtain justice, not only was no help at all when it did come, but it even increased sin. Evil human nature, consequently, becomes more hostile to it; the more the law forbids it to indulge its own desires, the more it wants to. Thus the law makes Christ all the more necessary and demands more grace to help human nature.

In chapter 6, St. Paul takes up the special work of faith, the struggle which the spirit wages against the flesh to kill off those sins and desires that remain after a person has been made just. He teaches us that faith doesn't so free us from sin that we can be idle, lazy and self-assured, as though there were no more sin in us. Sin *is* there, but, because of faith that struggles against it, God does not reckon sin as deserving damnation. Therefore we have in our own selves a lifetime of work cut out for us; we have to tame our body, kill its lusts, force its members to obey the spirit and not the lusts. We must do this so that we may conform to the death and resurrection of Christ and complete our Baptism, which signifies a death to sin and a new life of grace. Our aim is to be completely clean from sin and then to rise bodily with Christ and live forever.

St. Paul says that we can accomplish all this because we are in grace and not in the law. He explains that to be "outside the law" is not the same as having no law and being able to do what you please. No, being "under the law" means living without grace, surrounded by the works of the law. Then surely sin reigns by means of the law, since no one is naturally well-disposed toward the law. That very condition, however, is the greatest sin. But grace makes the law lovable to us, so there is then no sin any more, and the law is no longer against us but one with us.

This is true freedom from sin and from the law; St. Paul writes about this for the rest of the chapter. He says it is a freedom only to do good with eagerness and to live a good life without the coercion of the law. This freedom is, therefore, a spiritual freedom which does not suspend the law but which supplies what the law demands, namely eagerness and love. These silence the law so that it has no further cause to drive people on and make demands of them. It's as though you owed something to a moneylender and couldn't pay him. You could be rid of him in one of two ways: either he would take nothing from you and would tear up his account book, or a pious man would pay for you and give you what you needed to satisfy your debt. That's exactly how Christ freed us from the law. Therefore our freedom is not a wild, fleshy freedom that has no obligation to do anything. On the contrary, it is a freedom that does a great deal, indeed everything, yet is free of the law's demands and debts.

In chapter 7, St. Paul confirms the foregoing by an analogy drawn from married life. When a man dies, the wife is free; the one is free and clear of the other. It is not the case that the woman may not or should not marry another man; rather she is now for the first time free to marry someone else. She could not do this before she was free of her first husband. In the same way, our conscience is bound to the law so long as our condition is that of the sinful old man. But when the old man is killed by the spirit, then the conscience is free, and conscience and law are quit of each other. Not that conscience should now do nothing; rather, it should now for the first time truly cling to its second husband, Christ, and bring forth the fruit of life.

Next St. Paul sketches further the nature of sin and the law. It is the law that makes sin really active and powerful, because the old man gets more and more hostile to the law since he can't pay the debt demanded by the law. Sin is his very nature; of himself he can't do otherwise. And so the law is his death and torture. Now the law is not itself evil; it is our evil nature that cannot tolerate that the good law should demand good from it. It's like the case of a sick person, who cannot tolerate that you demand that he run and jump around and do other things that a healthy person does.

St. Paul concludes here that, if we understand the law properly and comprehend it in the best possible way, then we will see that its sole function is to remind us of our sins, to kill us by our sins, and to make us deserving of eternal wrath. Conscience learns and experiences all this in detail when it comes face to face with the law. It follows, then, that we must have something else, over and above the law, which can make a person virtuous and cause him to be saved. Those, however, who do not understand the law rightly are blind; they go their way boldly and think they are satisfying the law with works. They don't know how much the law demands, namely, a free, willing, eager heart. That is the reason that they don't see Moses rightly before their eyes. [In both Jewish and Christian teaching, Moses was commonly held to be the author of the Pentateuch, the first five books of the bible. Cf. the involved imagery of Moses' face and the veil over it in 2 Corinthians 3:7-18.] For them he is covered and concealed by the veil.

Then St. Paul shows how spirit and flesh struggle with each other in one person. He gives himself as an example, so that we may learn how to kill sin in ourselves. He gives both spirit and flesh the name "law," so that, just as it is in the nature of divine law to drive a person on and make demands of him, so too the flesh drives and demands and rages against the spirit and wants to have its own way. Likewise the spirit drives and demands against the flesh and wants to have its own way. This feud lasts in us for as long as we live, in one person more, in another less, depending on whether spirit or flesh is stronger. Yet the whole human being is both: spirit and flesh. The human being fights with himself until he becomes completely spiritual.

In chapter 8, St. Paul comforts fighters such as these and tells them that this flesh will not bring them condemnation. He goes on to show what the nature of flesh and spirit are. Spirit, he says, comes from Christ, who has given us his Holy Spirit; the Holy Spirit makes us spiritual and restrains the flesh. The Holy Spirit assures us that we are God's children no matter how furiously sin may rage within us, so long as we follow the Spirit and struggle against sin in order to kill it. Because nothing is so effective in deadening the flesh as the cross and suffering, Paul comforts us in our suffering. He says that the Spirit, [cf. previous note about the meaning of "spirit."] love and all creatures will stand by us; the Spirit in us groans and all creatures long with us that we be freed from the flesh and from sin. Thus we see that these three chapters, 6, 7 and 8, all deal with the one work of faith, which is to kill the old Adam and to constrain the flesh.

In chapters 9, 10 and 11, St. Paul teaches us about the eternal providence of God. It is the original source which determines who would believe and who wouldn't, who can be set free from sin and who cannot. Such matters have been taken out of our hands and are put into God's hands so that we might become virtuous. It is absolutely necessary that it be so, for we are so weak and unsure of ourselves that, if it depended on us, no human being would be saved. The devil would overpower all of us. But God is steadfast; his providence will not fail, and no one can prevent its realization. Therefore we have hope against sin.

But here we must shut the mouths of those sacriligeous and arrogant spirits who, mere beginners that they are, bring their reason to bear on this matter and commence, from their exalted position, to probe the abyss of divine providence and uselessly trouble themselves about whether they are predestined or not. These people must surely plunge to their ruin, since they will either despair or abandon themselves to a life of chance.

You, however, follow the reasoning of this letter in the order in which it is presented. Fix your attention first of all on Christ and the Gospel, so that you may recognize your sin and his grace. Then struggle against sin, as chapters 1-8 have taught you to. Finally, when you have come, in chapter 8, under the shadow of the cross and suffering, they will teach you, in chapters 9-11, about providence and what a comfort it is. [The context here and in St. Paul's letter makes it clear that this is the cross and passion, not only of Christ, but of each Christian.] Apart from suffering, the cross and the pangs of death, you cannot come to grips with providence without harm to yourself and secret anger against God. The old Adam must be quite dead before you can endure this matter and drink this strong wine. Therefore make sure you don't drink wine while you are still a babe at the breast. There is a proper measure, time and age for understanding every doctrine.

In chapter 12, St. Paul teaches the true liturgy and makes all Christians priests, so that they may offer, not money or cattle, as priests do in the Law, but their own bodies, by putting their desires to death. Next he describes the outward conduct of Christians whose lives are governed by the Spirit; he tells how they teach, preach, rule, serve, give, suffer, love, live and act toward friend, foe and everyone. These are the works that a Christian does, for, as I have said, faith is not idle.

In chapter 13, St. Paul teaches that one should honor and obey the secular authorities. He includes this, not because it makes people virtuous in the sight of God, but because it does insure that the virtuous have outward peace and protection and that the wicked cannot do evil without fear and in undisturbed peace. Therefore it is the duty of virtuous people to honor secular authority, even though they do not, strictly speaking, need it. Finally, St. Paul sums up everything in love and gathers it all into the example of Christ: what he has done for us, we must also do and follow after him.

In chapter 14, St. Paul teaches that one should carefully guide those with weak conscience and spare them. One shouldn't use Christian freedom to harm but rather to help the weak. Where that isn't done, there follow dissention and despising of the Gospel, on which everything else depends. It is better to give way a little to the weak in faith until they become stronger than to have the teaching of the Gospel perish completely. This work is a particularly necessary work of love especially now when people, by eating meat and by other freedoms, are brashly, boldly and unnecessarily shaking weak consciences which have not yet come to know the truth.

In chapter 15, St. Paul cites Christ as an example to show that we must also have patience with the weak, even those who fail by sinning publicly or by their disgusting morals. We must not cast them aside but must bear with them until they become better. That is the way Christ treated us and still treats us every day; he puts up with our vices, our wicked morals and all our imperfection, and he helps us ceaselessly. Finally Paul prays for the Christians at Rome; he praises them and commends them to God. He points out his own office and the message that he preaches. He makes an unobtrusive plea for a contribution for the poor in Jerusalem. Unalloyed love is the basis of all he says and does.

The last chapter consists of greetings. But Paul also includes a salutary warning against human doctrines which are preached alongside the Gospel and which do a great deal of harm. It's as though he had clearly seen that out of Rome and through the Romans would come the deceitful, harmful Canons and Decretals along with the entire brood and swarm of human laws and commands that is now drowning the whole world and has blotted out this letter and the whole of the Scriptures, along with the Spirit and faith. Nothing remains but the idol Belly, and St. Paul depicts those people here as its servants. God deliver us from them. Amen.

We find in this letter, then, the richest possible teaching about what a Christian should know: the meaning of law, Gospel, sin, punishment, grace, faith, justice, Christ, God, good works, love, hope and the cross. We learn how we are to act toward everyone, toward the virtuous and sinful, toward the strong and the weak, friend and foe, and toward ourselves. Paul bases everything firmly on Scripture and proves his points with examples from his own experience and from the Prophets, so that nothing more could be desired. Therefore it seems that St. Paul, in writing this letter, wanted to compose a summary of the whole of Christian and evangelical teaching which would also be an introduction to the whole Old Testament. Without doubt, whoever takes this letter to heart possesses the light and power of the Old Testament. Therefore each and every Christian should make this letter the habitual and constant object of his study. God grant us his grace to do so. Amen.

John Calvin's Seal

1509-1564 A.D.

Rev. Jim Thompson to Henry Willet

"The sanctuary windows are magnificent and almost breath-taking to behold. The lancets on each side of the doors are also good-except that you kept Calvin's coat of arms. Shame on you."

Throughout the construction of the windows Rev. Thompson and Henry Willet, an elder in the Presbyterian Church, interposed playful banter with candidness in their correspondence.

John Calvin's Seal and Motto

The stained glass panel is a representation of John Calvin's seal. The design of the seal itself is a hand holding out a heart, appearing to present it to someone out of view. It is likely that Calvin designed it as a depiction of him presenting his heart to God with outstretched hand, offering himself wholly to Him. Evidence supporting this assertion can be found in a letter to a colleague, Farel, where Calvin related his concern about returning to Geneva to take up the work of reform there after being asked to leave years before. Calvin wrote, "When I remember that in this matter I am not my own master, I present my heart as a sacrifice and offer it up to the Lord." This statement correlates with the design of Calvin's seal and reveals the depth of his determination to obey the will of God. In addition, it demonstrates an expression of modesty and genuine humility, and a confession of uncertainty, which is further connected by the motto borne on the seal: My heart I offer to thee, O Lord, promptly and sincerely (*Cor Meum Tibi Offero Domine Prompte Et Sincere)*.[1]

When Calvin's theology is recognized as a humble confessional exposition of the gospel rather than a triumphant explanation of it, the angle at which this vision comes is inescapably shifted. Calvin as a theologian was aware that he could only describe the edges and not the essence of God's mystery. He contended theology did not present the truth, but sought to protect the Truth as revealed in Jesus Christ. Of course, similar to most theologians, Calvin tried to balance head, heart, and hand. Even so, Calvin insisted, theological witness came from the human heart, not merely the head. As he stated in the *Institutes,* the gospel "is a doctrine not of the tongue but of life. It is not apprehended by the understanding and memory alone, as other disciplines are, but it is received only when it possesses the whole soul, and finds a seat and resting place in the inmost affection of the heart."[2] John Calvin may be seen, therefore, as a theologian of the heart—a subject reflected very powerfully by Calvin's seal.

John (Jean) Calvin (1509-1564

John (Jean) Calvin was born July 10, 1509, in Noyon, France, and raised in a staunch Roman Catholic family. His father, Gerard Calvin, was an administrator in the town's cathedral and wanted his son, Jean, to become a priest. At the age of 14, Calvin went to Paris to study at the Collège de la Marche in preparation for university study in divinity. Calvin stayed closely tied to the Roman Catholic church during his studies, but he did befriend some reform-minded individuals. One professor, a Latin scholar, Maturin Cordier, introduced Calvin to the scholarly pursuit of humanism—the study of classical antiquity, culture, literature, and moral philosophy, particularly Greek and Roman—which would inform much of his successive learning. Calvin was relatively close to a number of his other humanist professors, in addition to his reform-minded friends. Cordier and these other contacts would set the stage for Calvin's eventual conversion to the Protestant faith.[3]

By 1528, Calvin moved to Orleans to study law, after advice from his father that to study law rather than theology would be a surer road to success. In 1532, Calvin finished his law studies and earned a doctorate in civil law. In the same year, he published his first book, a commentary on a work by the Roman philosopher, Seneca, that demonstrated not only his vast knowledge and training in both the classics and Renaissance humanism, but also his belief in moral education, and his devotion to antiquity.[4] Between 1532 and 1534, Calvin's views changed and he converted to Protestantism. As he described in a commentary on the Psalms in 1557, "It would have been hard indeed to have pulled me out of so deep a quagmire by a sudden conversion. But God subdued and made teachable a heart which, for my age, was far too hardened in such matters."[5] His ministry as a reformer would often be the struggle to subdue and make teachable undisciplined and hardened hearts.

Returning to Noyon in 1534, Calvin seemingly was troubled by the native French reform movement and its failure to implement its beliefs and bring about actual reform. These two concepts—internal belief and external action—comprised what would become the hallmark of Calvinism. His new-found faith prompted the work, *Institutes of the Christian Religion*, which would earn him an international reputation. The *Institutes* was written to "aid those who desire[d] to be instructed in the doctrine of salvation."[6] Divided into four parts, the *Institutes* examined God, the Father; the Son; the Holy Spirit; and the Church. By its final edition in 1559, the *Institutes* would be a comprehensive statement of Reformed Protestantism.[7] The Reformed tradition within the Protestant Church was distinguished by its origin in the Swiss

Reformation, its adherence to Calvinist doctrine, and its independence in church governmental organization. Calvinism also gave social and political activism a theological importance, whereas others did not.

By 1536, Calvin disengaged himself from the Roman Catholic Church and made plans to permanently leave France. Planning a one-night stay in Geneva en route to Strasbourg to live a scholarly life, Calvin ended up staying in Geneva off and on the rest of his life. He arrived in Geneva to find a city that had undergone some significant religious and political upheaval in recent years that had resulted in Geneva's political independence from overlords. The city's people had also just pledged to accept the Reformation—a religious movement brought about at least in part by unresolved religious oppression and the articulation thereof by a monk, Martin Luther. As the city began its new religious journey, Farel, a Protestant preacher and local reformer, recognized Calvin and asked him to stay and join in the work to reform the city. With a sense of duty, Calvin agreed. Almost overnight, Calvin assumed leadership of the Geneva Reformation.[8]

The following year, Calvin laid the groundwork and spelled out for the Genevans what he thought their religious lives, duties, and governance should involve. He and Farel were to devise a reform too radical for the Geneva people, who had just liberated themselves politically and religiously from external control. In 1538, Calvin and Farel were asked to leave the city. Calvin then settled in Strasbourg, his original destination in 1536, and became a lecturer in the university, living there for the next three years. While in Strasbourg, Calvin finished the second edition of the *Institutes* and wrote his first Biblical commentary on Paul's letter to the Romans. The leader of the Strasbourg clergy, Martin Bucer, would be extremely influential in Calvin's development concerning church government and worship and overall as a Protestant reformer, concepts he would carry back to Geneva.[9]

In 1541, Calvin returned to the city at the request of the Council of Geneva. Having learned from his mistakes when in Geneva earlier, Calvin demonstrated a respect for the political sovereignty of the city over that of the clergy. He would successfully oversee the implementation of a new ecclesiastical ordinance and issuance of the *Geneva Catechism* later that year. The influx of large numbers of religious refugees into Geneva and the political defeat of Calvin's political opponents in the mid-1550s combined to stabilize and secure his influence in the city. In 1559, Calvin became a citizen and developed a new school system, the Geneva Academy. The system consisted of a primary school of seven grades and the academy proper, which provided theological training for an international population.[10] The Academy would become the intellectual training ground for Protestant leadership in the second half of the sixteenth century. Calvin would remain in Geneva until his death in 1564.

1. Philip Schaff, "Calvin's Recall to Geneva," in *History of the Christian Church, Volume VIII: Modern Christianity, The Swiss Reformation*. Third Edition, Revised .

2. John Calvin, in The *Institutes of the Christian Religion*.

3. Henry Collin Minton, "John Calvin, Lawyer" in *The North American Review*, vol. 190, no. 645, August 1909, pp212-221.

4. Steven Ozment, *The Age of Reform: 1250-1550, An Intellectual and Religious History of Late Medieval And Renaissance Europe;* Robert D. Linder, "Calvin and Humanism: The First Generation" in *Church History*, vol. 44, no. 2, Jun 1975, pp 167-181.

5. Francois Wendel, as quoted by Ozment.

6. John Calvin, "Subject of the Present Work," in The *Institutes of the Christian Religion*.

7. Ozment, *The Age of Reform*; John H. Leith, *Introduction to the Reformed Tradition*.

8. Ozment, *The Age of Reform*.

9. Ibid.

10. Ibid.

Andi Knecht

WESLEY COAT OF ARMS

The Wesley Coat of Arms found in the stained glass window panel at the right entrance of the Gainesville First United Methodist Church is a shield containing a cross with five scallop shells on the cross. It appears to be a simplified version of an engraving by James Fittler of a portrait of John Wesley which hangs in the National Portrait Gallery in London. Beneath the portrait Fittler added his conception of the Wesley family Coat of Arms which was a shield with an outlined cross which contains three scallop shells in each quarter and a dragon with wings and a barbed tail. The words, "God is love" is the motto underneath. Whether John Wesley approved this drawing is not known, but Wesley did use the words "God is love" on one of his seals and the Coat of Arms underneath the portrait is a representation which appears in Methodism. The scallop shell is thought to mean that one of Wesley's ancestors had been a crusader and a pilgrim to the Holy Land. In the Middle Ages the shell became a religious emblem known as the badge of St. James and was worn by pilgrims visiting the shrine of St. James in Spain and the Holy Land. The shrine in Spain is known as Santiago de Compostela ("The field of the star of St. James"). It is said that a shepherd in the year 813 saw a star shining down on an oak tree and followed the light to the tree and there he saw bones which local bishops declared were the remains of the disciple St. James. A cathedral was built on the spot where the bones were found and this church became a pilgrimage site for Christians although modern scholars are doubtful about the authenticity of the story. The scallop shell later came to symbolize anyone who had made long journeys or voyages to foreign countries. Through Wesley's Coat of Arms we are linked to all who join in the quest for Christ. Methodism can be traced back to John Wesley's journey to the colony of Georgia in the 1730s which led to his own "faith journey." He had a crisis of faith before he went to the colony and the failure of his mission in Georgia added to his feeling of spiritual despair. It was in this state of mind and emotion that he attended a Moravian meeting on Aldersgate Street in London in 1738 and heard a reading of Martin Luther's preface to the Epistle to the Romans. Upon hearing the reading, Wesley's heart was "strangely warmed" and he underwent a transformation that caused him to lead a reform movement within the Church of England that culminated in the creation of Methodism and the establishment of an autonomous American Methodist Episcopal Church after his death. Thus the symbolism and message found in the Wesley Coat of Arms is inextricably related to John Wesley's journey to Georgia and his personal journey of faith which transformed him from one with self-doubts to a believer in salvation through faith by God's grace and not good works. His story is a remarkable one as we will see.

JOHN WESLEY (1703-1791)

Born in 1703 in Epworth, England, John Wesley led an effort to reform the Church of England in the 18th century which resulted in a separate movement known as Methodism and an autonomous American Methodist Episcopal Church after his death. Wesley was the 15th of 19 children born to Anglican rector Samuel Wesley and his wife Susanna. At the age of five, the young John was thought to have perished in a fire that burned the rectory. To Susanna, the miraculous rescue was a sign that the boy was special and that God had important plans for his life. Upon seeing him, she quoted from Zechariah 3:2 saying that he was set apart as a "brand plucked from the burning." Wesley went on to be educated at Oxford and ordained a deacon in the Church of England in 1725 and the next year elected a fellow of Lincoln College, Oxford. He was ordained as a priest in the Church in 1728.

At Oxford, Methodism had its earliest roots in the Holy Club organized by Wesley's younger brother Charles and fellow students including George Whitefield. John joined this group of students who followed a very systematic routine of prayer, receiving communion, reading the scriptures and ministering to the poor and sick as well as to those imprisoned. They were mockingly referred to as "Methodists" because of their routine and methodical religious practices. Wesley was a zealous servant of God but like Martin Luther two centuries earlier he had grave doubts about his salvation and felt he did not have the faith to continue preaching.

In 1735 a significant event occurred in Wesley's life. He and Charles were invited by James Oglethorpe to accompany him to Georgia, the colony that Oglethorpe founded in 1733. They were to be ministers to the colonists and hopefully to the Native Americans there. On the voyage across the Atlantic to the colony Wesley met a band of German Moravians on board who during a violent storm that threatened to overturn the ship remained calm singing hymns and uttering prayers. Wesley saw that they had a faith and an inner strength that he did not have. In the face of death, he was afraid and found little comfort in his religion. In Georgia, Wesley met and fell in love with Sophia Hopkey, the young niece of the chief magistrate of the colony. This relationship proved his undoing there when she married another man before he could tell her of his affections. Distraught, a mean-spirited Wesley excluded Sophia and her husband from communion. A suit was brought against him for defaming her character. Wesley felt this was a church matter and should not be brought before the magistrates. Nonetheless, a grand jury indicted him and John and Charles left the colony in 1737 having failed in their efforts there.

However, from this failure Methodism took form. Wesley remembered his experience with the Moravians and he turned to them in his state of depression, defeat and self-doubt. He attended a Moravian meeting on Aldersgate Street in London on May 24, 1738. This was the occasion of his famous "Aldersgate experience" in which, after hearing a reading of Martin Luther's preface to the Epistle to the Romans, he underwent a sudden transformation. He later wrote in his diary the well-known lines, "...about a quarter before nine, while the reader was describing the change which God works in the heart through faith in Christ, I felt my heart strangely warmed." He went on to write, "I felt I did trust in Christ, Christ alone, for salvation; and an assurance was given me that He had taken away *my* sins, even *mine*, and saved *me* from the law of sin and death." Luther's emphasis on Justification by Faith made a deep impression on Wesley and dramatically changed his life and the character and method of his ministry. He saw that it is not Christ and good works, but Christ alone who saves; good works would follow. He began preaching sermons on the doctrine of salvation by faith and other sermons on God's grace. Charles was reported to have undergone a similar conversion earlier. John found himself being excluded from many pulpits because of his sermons. His friend George Whitefield who had replaced him in Georgia was also barred from pulpits because of a "conversion experience" similar to Wesley's when he returned to Bristol, England. Not to be deterred, Whitefield began preaching in the open air to the working class in Bristol who lived in very poor conditions. Whitefield invited Wesley to emulate his method of preaching which Wesley reluctantly did in 1739 beginning the Methodist movement. Wesley realized that outdoor preaching was a successful way of reaching those who had been neglected by the Church of England. The country was in the beginning of the Industrial Revolution which led to men, women and children working in factories under wretched conditions and living in substandard tenement housing. Wesley and Whitefield preached wherever a crowd gathered. Wesley even preached using his father's tombstone as a pulpit. The two men were very successful as those who felt ignored by the Church flocked to the new movement. However, Wesley broke with Whitefield over the latter's belief in predestination; Wesley believed that the love of God was universal and that because of that love He would not save some from sin and damn others.

Wesley was assisted by his brother Charles in the new movement. Charles added an important dimension to the revival movement writing more than 6,000 hymns which expressed the two messages of God's assurance of salvation to all who earnestly repented their sins and the power of the Holy Spirit to enable all to attain perfect love for God. Thus began the rich musical tradition in Methodism; the singing of hymns then as now is an essential part of worship services.

Even though Wesley utilized nonconformist methods to get his message to the people and he disagreed with the apathy of the Church, its corrupt clergy, its attitude toward the salvation of its parishioners and its regulations about who had authority to preach, Wesley wished to remain within the Church of

England which he felt was "...nearer the Scriptural plans than any other in Europe." The relationship to the Church remained strained, however, as Wesley and his clergy found themselves under attack by the Church. Nonetheless, Wesley felt called by God to lead a revival in the Church and nothing would stop him.

As the movement grew, Wesley needed additional preachers to help with his revival movement so he approved local preachers who were not ordained by the Anglican Church to preach and to do pastoral work. The use of lay preachers was an integral part of the new Methodist reform movement. Wesley also utilized the itinerant method of sending preachers to specific circuits and changing the preachers to different circuits every two years or so to improve their efficiency and effectiveness. Itinerancy would remain an important part of Methodism down to the present. He had established the first Methodist conference in 1744 in London for discussion of doctrinal and administrative purposes. The use of conferences is still a part of the Methodist Church.

Methodist preachers were sent to the American colonies before the War for Independence separated the colonies from Great Britain. In 1784, after independence the American Methodists who chose not to return to England were without the sacraments and needed an ordained minister to administer them. A concerned Wesley in a very bold move ordained Thomas Coke, already an Anglican priest, and appointed him superintendent of Methodists in America. Coke in turn ordained Francis Asbury and the two ordained others in the new American Methodist Episcopal Church in the United States. Wesley had come to the conclusion that the concept of apostolic succession whereby only bishops could ordain priests was not biblically based. This concept had been an important part of the Catholic Church going back to early Christianity with St. Peter seen as the first bishop, the Bishop of Rome. The Church of England had adopted it in its beginning. Charles felt that his brother's actions would end his and John's relationship with the Anglican Church, but it did not and John remained an Anglican priest until his death in 1791. He was very happy about the new Methodist Church in America but he remained and died in the established church. John left behind a tremendous legacy. Through his tireless efforts countless individuals were won to Christ. It is said that during the course of his revival movement he rode on horseback some 250,000 miles up and down the roads and pathways of his native country and preached more than 10,000 sermons.

The Methodist Church today reflects the beliefs, practices and methods of Wesley's ministry as well as the contributions of his brother Charles. Methodism remains committed to a social imperative that works toward the inclusiveness of God's love. Wesley said, "I look at all the world as my parish...." Methodists believe that Christ died for all of humanity, not simply for a few, and this means every person is entitled to God's grace. Wesley took the message to all including the poor, the uneducated, the criminal and others outside organized religion. This practice is still a part of Methodism. Itinerancy was utilized in America with preachers riding circuits on horseback in the early days and ministers still are moved by bishops to different appointments. Bishops remain spiritual and administrative heads of conferences within states and Methodist jurisdictions. John and Charles Wesley left an indelible mark on Methodism not only in America but throughout the world where Methodism is found.

James Southerland

"About 3:30 in the afternoon I first set foot on St. Simons Island and immediately my spirits revived."
Charles Wesley, March 9, 1736.

Georgia Historical Marker –Sea Island, Georgia

The Reverends John & Charles Wesley marker & the Wesley Memorial Garden is located on the east side of Fort Frederica Road at the Wesley Memorial Garden, just south of the entrance to Fort Frederica, St. Simons Island, GA.

Ordained ministers of the Anglican Church, the Wesleys joined General James Oglethorpe, founder and first Governor of Georgia on his second trip to Georgia. John Wesley is remembered as the founder of Methodism. His brother Charles is remembered as a prolific poet and writer of over 6,000 hymns.
John Wesley was authorized by the Trustees of the Colony of Georgia to perform religious and ecclesiastical offices in the colony. Charles Wesley was to be secretary of Indian Affairs and to perform religious duties at Frederica.
Both had some bitter experiences and believed their ministry in Georgia was a failure. However, history has proved otherwise. Their work in Georgia is called the second rise of Methodism; the first being with the Holy Club in England.
The Wesley Memorial Garden is a place where people may experience the same revival of the spirit felt by Charles Wesley when he arrived on St. Simons Island and when John Wesley felt his heart strangely warmed during his Aldersgate experience in London on May 24, 1738

The history and significance of the Cross and Flame emblem are as rich and diverse as The United Methodist Church. The insignia's birth quickly followed the union of two denominations in 1968: The Methodist Church and the Evangelical United Brethren Church.

Following more than two dozen conceptualizations, a traditional symbol—the cross—was linked with a single flame with dual tongues of fire. The resulting insignia is rich in meaning. It relates The United Methodist church to God through Christ (cross) and the Holy Spirit (flame). The flame is a reminder of Pentecost when witnesses were unified by the power of the Holy Spirit and saw "tongues, as of fire" (Acts 2:3).

The elements of the emblem also remind us of a transforming moment in the life of Methodism's founder, John Wesley, when he sensed God's presence and felt his heart "strangely warmed." The two tongues of a single flame may also be understood to represent the union of two denominations. (umc.org)

This corner stone of the Old Green St. Church reads: The First Methodist Episcopal Church-South.

The Methodist Episcopal Church was founded in 1784 with Francis Asbury and Thomas Coke as the first bishops. In 1939 it merged with the Methodist Episcopal Church, South and the Methodist Protestant Church to form the Methodist Church. In 1968 it merged with the Evangelical United Brethren Church to form the present United Methodist Church.

Charles Wesley

1707-1788

Songs of Our Faith

The industrial revolution in England was a turbulent time for many. John and Charles Wesley, founders of the Methodist movement, lived during this time. They were ministers in the Church of England but spent most of their years in the mission field, both there and, briefly, in America.

John was a preacher. He brought the gospel of Jesus to the masses, preaching in churches when possible, but often in the town green or in the fields nearby. Brother Charles was also a preacher, but we remember him more for his prolific output of hymn texts. During his years of ministry he is thought to have written over 6000 hymns.

The Wesleys produced some our earliest songbooks, designed for use in their travels through England. These were pocket size pamphlets that were carried to the meetings and passed out for people to keep. Later hymnals were designed for the same use, carried by circuit riding preachers to their scattered flocks in America.

Our heritage of hymns is rich indeed, with many of Charles' texts in common use in hymnals of every major denomination, even after two hundred years. Set to noble hymn tunes and harmonies, Wesley hymns convey the bedrock of Methodist theology and belief.

Spend some time reading the texts and absorb their meaning. You can find them all in the *Index of Composers, Authors, and Sources* in the 1989 *United Methodist Hymnal,* page 922.

Hoping to whet your appetite I would recommend starting with No. 384, *Love Divine, All Loves Excelling.* The four stanzas of this great hymn concisely convey the foundation of Christian faith. Here is the majestic final stanza:

> *Finish, then thy new creation; pure and spotless let us be.*
> *Let us see thy great salvation perfectly restored in thee;*
> *changed from glory into glory, till in heaven we take our place,*
> *till we cast our crowns before thee, lost in wonder, love and praise.*

Sam Marley

157

Hark! The Herald Angels Sing!

One of the earliest hymns of the Christian Church is the Doxology mentioned in Luke 2:14 – "Glory to God in the Highest." These words were sung or spoken by the angels to announce the birth of Christ. Over the years this hymn was rendered in Greek and in Latin versions, the latter being most familiar to us as the "Gloria in excelsis deo." In contemporary liturgical services such as are found in the Episcopal, Lutheran and Catholic churches, the hymn maintains a position of great importance and prominence.

During the Protestant Reformation, hymn writers in England, Germany, and other countries looked for ways to adapt some of these Latin hymns into other languages. Martin Luther was one of the most prolific individuals at making adaptations. But many others followed, however, and Charles Wesley was certainly influenced by these.

The carol we know and love today as "Hark! The herald angels sing" did not start out that way. It is interesting to note that at least four people were involved in its inception and transformation: Charles Wesley, George Whitefield, Felix Mendelssohn, and William Cummings.

Wesley's original text was written as a Christmas Day hymn and first published in 1739. It is made up of ten four-line verses, rather than the longer eight-line verses with refrain which we have now. His original opens with the phrase "Hark? how all the welkin rings / Glory to the King of Kings." Welkin is an old English word that refers to the sky, firmament, or heavens.

George Whitefield, who had known Wesley as a student at Oxford University, changed the first phrase to that which we know today: "Hark! The herald angels sing / Glory to the newborn King." Thus Wesley's original text which echoed Luke's "Glory to God in the highest heaven" was changed forever. Whitefield went on to make additional alterations in the number and length of Wesley's verses.

Wesley had suggested that a "slow, solemn tune" would best suit the text. However, the tune we associate with the hymn was adapted by an English composer, William Cummings, from music by Felix Mendelssohn. Mendelssohn's music had originally been written for a cantata to celebrate the invention of the printing press by Johann Gutenberg.

Thus we find that this remarkable and much-beloved carol, without which no Christmas music program could possibly exist, has a storied heritage. Isn't it amazing that Charles Wesley's hymn text took its inspiration from the Christmas story in St. Luke's gospel. Mendelssohn's music seems "made" for the text. But, were it not for the good work of Whitefield and Cummings, this glorious marriage of word and music might never have survived the centuries!

James F. Mellichamp

The Treble Clef

The Role of Music in Worship

The treble clef is one of the oldest and most recognizable symbols of music notation. It spirals around the second line from the bottom of the staff to identify G above middle C, and its main purpose is to serve as a guide to help musicians read the notes on the staff. It has served this function for hundreds of years, though music certainly developed for millennia as an oral tradition passed down from one generation to the next before written music existed.

Music has long been an important aspect of worship. The treble clef in the stained glass windows of our church reminds us of this. Numerous passages in the Old Testament describe how people praised god with instruments and their voices.

First Chronicles 15:22 – "And Chenaniah, chief of the Levites, was in charge of the singing; he gave instruction in singing because he was skillful."

The Levites were very skilled in music making, and Second Chronicles 34:12 also speaks of Levites who were skillful playing musical instruments. Not only were they very talented, but there many of them as well. First Chronicles 23:5 identifies 4,000 who praised God with instruments. Can you imagine trying to conduct such a large orchestra, especially without the modern facilities and technology we have today?

Many passages in the Psalms instruct us to praise God with music, which in many ways goes beyond speaking in expressing feelings of the heart, mind and soul.

Psalms 98:4 – "Make a joyful noise unto the Lord…."

Psalms 98:4 – "O sing unto the Lord a new song; … make a joyful noise unto the Lord.

Psalms 105:2 – "Sing unto him, sing psalms unto him…."

Psalm 150:3–4 "Praise Him with trumpet sound; praise Him with harp and lyre. Praise Him with timbrel and dancing; praise Him with stringed instruments and pipe."

Although not referenced as frequently, there are also a number of scriptures in the New Testament that attest to music as a form of praise and worship:

Mark 14:26 – "And after Jesus and the twelve had partaken of the last supper, they sang a hymn."

Ephesians 5:18–19 – "Be filled with the Spirit, speaking to one another in psalms and hymns and spiritual songs, singing and making melody with your heart to the Lord."

Revelation 14:1-3 – And I looked, and, lo, a Lamb stood on the Mount Sion, and with him an hundred forty and four thousand, ... and they sung as it were a new song before the throne, ... and no man could learn that song but the hundred and forty and four thousand, which were redeemed from the earth."

Music has continued to be an integral part of worship throughout the history of modern church. The singing of hymns and other songs helps us learn scripture and spiritual truths. It also enables us to lift our emotions to God in a way spoken word doesn't.

There are several aspects of music that enhance the worship experience significantly. As you enter worship Sunday mornings, think about the music you hear before the service begins. Its purpose is to establish the mood and help us prepare our hearts and minds for worship. During the service, music affords us an opportunity for collective participation. We spend a significant amount of time as observers, but music allows us to get involved in ways of learning and praising God and recalling scripture.

When a soloist, choir or praise team perform, they invite listeners to hear a proclamation of the gospel or testimony that connects emotionally with the performers themselves. This expression of faith reaches out to the congregation and invites them to share and celebrate the message.

How often do you focus your attention to the words of the songs or hymns we sing in church every Sunday? When singing the Doxology or any commonly performed congregational song, think about the text and try expressing the emotional context the composer intended for us.

Praise God, from whom all blessings flow; praise him, all creatures here below;
Praise him above, ye heavenly host; praise Father, Son, and Holy Ghost. Amen.

John LaForge
GFUMC Director of Worship Arts

Francis Asbury

1745-1816

Francis Asbury on a horse and in front of an opened bible-Asbury was a circuit rider and the General Superintendent of the Methodist Societies in the United States of America. He was responsible for the great spread of the denomination in this country.

In 1790 Asbury established Bethel Academy in central Kentucky. The Methodist school, the first of its kind west of the Allegheny Mountains, was located three and a half miles south of the present day town of Wilmore, Kentucky. This local connection, the fact that Bethel Academy was founded exactly one hundred years before, and most importantly the theological similarities, led to the Kentucky Holiness College being renamed Asbury College in 1891.

Francis Asbury, the "Father of American Methodism," was born at Hamstead Bridge, Staffordshire, England. His parents were poor, so he dropped out of school at age fourteen to help support the family. At age thirteen, he had been converted to Methodism, and at age sixteen he became a local preacher. He was a simple, fluent speaker, and was so successful that in 1767 he was enrolled, by John Wesley himself, as a regular itinerant minister. In 1771 he volunteered for missionary work in the American colonies and when he arrived in Philadelphia in October 1771, the Methodist converts totaled approximately 300. Asbury infused new life into the movement and doubled the membership within his first year in the colonies.

After the outbreak of the War of Independence, the Methodists, who then numbered several thousands, fell, unjustly, under suspicion of Loyalism, mainly because of their refusal to take the prescribed oath. Many of their ministers returned to England. Asbury, however, feeling his sympathies and duties to be with the colonies, remained at his post, and although often threatened, and once arrested, continued his itinerant preaching.

In 1784 John Wesley, in disregard of the authority of the established Anglican Church of England, took the radical step of appointing the Rev. Thomas Coke and Francis Asbury superintendents or "bishops" of the church in the United States. Coke was ordained at Bristol, England in September, and in the following December, in a conference of the churches in America at Baltimore, he ordained and consecrated Asbury, who refused to accept the position until Wesley's choice had been ratified by the conference. This conference dates the beginning of the "Methodist Episcopal Church of the United States of America." To the upbuilding of this church Asbury dedicated the rest of his life, working with tireless devotion and great energy. Every year Asbury traversed a large area, mostly on horseback and by carriage. The greatest testimony to the work that earned for him the title of the "Father of American Methodism" was the growth of the denomination, from a few scattered bands of about 300 converts and 4 preachers in 1771, to a thoroughly organized church of 214,000 members and more than 2000 ministers at his death in 1816. By the Civil War, American Methodists numbered 1.5 million with more than 4000 Methodist preachers.

Rev. Richard Pletsch

163

The Old Windows from the Green Street Church

Twelve stained glass windows were moved from the Green Street Church and stored in the North Wing of the new church. As moving from a church with so much history and memories was associated with nostalgic emotion, preserving the windows in many ways softened the transition to the Thompson Bridge location.

The windows were kept in crates in a wall, entombed so to speak, until the completion of the 1998 expansion. At this time eleven of the twelve were "excavated" and repaired by Llorens Leaded Glass Studio and used in the First United Methodist Church Chapel and Reception Hall. The Llorens Studio is a three generation company and had manufactured the original windows for the Green Street Church near the turn of the century.

There is a "Report on the Old Windows" by Henry Willet who was asked to assess the Old Windows as to their meaning and worth. In that report he mentions that one depicts a child pointing to the Fifth Commandment. This window was not used in the current church and still resides in a crate attached to a wall of our church for future use.

Rev. Thompson was fond of speaking from the pulpit and giving "window tours" about the figures in the windows and their meaning. In fact there was concern that without him many of their intricacies and history would be lost. On one such window tour a church member took notes as he went through the Sanctuary, Narthex and the new Chapel. These notes were given to Jackie Powers who in turn transcribed them. The following is what he said on one such tour regarding the old windows:

"Some of these windows are very old and from the early 1900's about the time the old Sanctuary was built. The Llorens Studio made these windows initially and then years later refurbished them to be used in the Chapel, the Chapel Narthex and in the Reception Hall."

Chapel Sanctuary-Above Altar

The Cross and Crown

2 Timothy 4:7-8

I have fought the good fight, I have finished the race, I have kept the faith. Now there is in store for me the crown of righteousness, which the Lord, the righteous Judge, will award to me on that day--and not only to me, but also to all who have longed for his appearing.

The cross represents our victory of faith in Christ, who by His atoning death gives to all believers eternal life – the Crown.

What the Windows See

I can see them from where I sit. They are innumerable, passing by in patterns as predictable as the rising and setting of the sun. Much about them has changed over the years here but one thing has remained the same. Whether driving, jogging or walking they are all driven. They are driven to succeed; they are driven to achieve prominence and prosperity. This drive is what wakes them early and holds them late. Off to work they go each morning to establish and protect their place in this noisy world. The return trip home is now much later than before. Longer hours at work mean larger wages. Larger wages mean more stuff. More stuff leads to bigger and better stuff. And of course he who amasses the most stuff of all is exalted above all of the others when is awarded the crown.

They do not know that I know why they do what they do. From where I sit I clearly see that they all, at least most of them, are driven by the inward desire for the crown. In their minds the crown is the final rung at the top of the proverbial ladder. The crown heralds, "I made it, I'm strong, I'm courageous, I'm mighty". They scurry to and fro quickly and I remain, day after day, perched above them like a lofty ideal. One quick glance, one somber look or curious gaze would allow them to see the simple truth.

Look at me closely and I will show you the truth. You can never have a crown without a cross. History is full of men who would become gods, but only one God who would become man. Many covet the crown yet despise the cross. You cannot have one without the other. Jesus is crowned King of kings and Lord of lords but one look at me reminds you that Jesus faced the cross before He would wear the crown. If only they would see me it would become clear. The surest way to an authentic crown is to embrace our personal cross and die to self that we might live out life for Him and for others.

Rev. Jeff Worley

The Cross and Crown windows are seen in the bell towers of the Old Green Street Church from the perspective of the Collegiate Grill.

166

Chapel-Left Side-Front to Back

The Angel Appears to the Shepherds

Luke 2: 8-12

And there were shepherds living out in the fields nearby, keeping watch over their flocks at night. An angel of the Lord appeared to them, and the glory of the Lord shone around them, and they were terrified. But the angel said to them, "Do not be afraid. I bring you good news that will cause great joy for all the people. Today in the town of David a Savior has been born to you; he is the Messiah, the Lord. This will be a sign to you: You will find a baby wrapped in cloths and lying in a manger."

I was seven years old the first time I saw this beautiful stained glass window of an angel appearing to shepherds. It was June 1962, and my father had just been appointed pastor of Gainesville First United Methodist Church. The move from Atlanta was my very first; my whole world had changed overnight.

While I remember looking at all of the stained glass windows in the sanctuary, studying each one closely, it was this one that caught my eye *and* my soul. Near the feet of the big angel, I noticed a little boy peeking from behind the angel's white robe. The boy seems afraid, but not so afraid to want to be left out of this new experience. I was immediately drawn to him. He depicted my own feelings of fear being in a new place, yet curious and excited about what was happening.

My parents could sense my unease as I studied the scene. At that moment, my mother reminded me of the scripture, "Do not fear!" — three words that can calm both storm and soul. To a scared little boy, those words were like dousing a hot fire with cool water. In that instant, my whole being began to relax.

Mother continued, "Do not fear, for behold I bring you good news of great joy. For unto you is born this day in the city of David, a savior who is Christ the Lord. This will be a sign for you: you will find a child wrapped in swaddling cloth, lying in a manger." That child, of course, would be called Emmanuel, which means "God is with us."

As a frightened little boy in a new church, new city, new home and soon-to-be new school, these words were life changing for me. God is with **ME**... do not fear! Not only would fear be eliminated, it would be replaced by Good News!

Mother still was not finished with sharing Luke's account of the birth of Jesus: "And suddenly there was with the angel a multitude of the heavenly host praising God and saying: 'Glory to God in the highest and on Earth peace to all.'"

Why would such angelic grandeur be directed toward "lowly" shepherds? After all, shepherds, at that time, were among the outcasts of society. They worked in the scorching sun for long periods at a time and their body odor was abysmal. They were marginalized by society and, even at seven years of age, I could relate to that. I, too, felt marginalized. As the new kid in an unfamiliar place, would I be accepted? What would my new world mean for me?

Yet, despite their standing in society, shepherds were the first ones to arrive at the manger; the story of Jesus's birth (and every Christmas pageant) would not be complete without them. They were the first evangelists to share transforming news with a world that never would be the same. These shepherds went from outcasts to being adored and imitated. Jesus, himself, eventually would say, "I am the Good Shepherd," and, today, many churches are even named for them.

At Christ's birth, the shepherds had a new song in their hearts — a song of acceptance, hope, peace, joy and the assurance of God's love. Indeed, in every generation since, those who experience the Christmas miracle have a new song in their hearts. With help from a stained glass window, Luke's account and my mother, I left the sanctuary that day with a new song in my own heart. It is the song that eliminates fear and replaces it with salvation and peace.

That was more than 50 years ago beneath this very special window, and that song has played for many people at many times and places since. May it continue to do so, again and again.

Dr. D. B. Shelnutt, Jr.

It was a Sunday afternoon service and at that time the pastor was Dumas Shelnutt (1962-1966). Rev. Shelnutt was in the pulpit and just as he was finishing a prayer, he looks up to see a paper airplane, constructed from the church bulletin, land perfectly at the altar in front of him. It seems a child had launched the plane from the balcony and it had traversed the entire length of the church before landing. There was a quiet unease throughout the congregation at witnessing this.

Without pause, Rev. Shelnutt says, "And might we say an additional prayer for the pilot of this plane."

Willis McLemore

The Good Shepherd

John 10:11

"I am the good shepherd. The good shepherd lays down his life for the sheep."

Psalm 23:1-2

A Psalm of David. The LORD is my shepherd, I shall not want. He makes me lie down in green pastures; He leads me beside quiet waters....

In memory of Dr. E. E. Dixon. 1846. 1903.

DIXON, Dr. E. E., died of Bright's disease at his home in
Gainesville this morning (date not stated); he was born in
Meriwether county in 1847, a son of the late Hon. J. L. Dixon
of Woodbury; he was a brother of Dr. J. T. and Mr. A. P. Dixon,
present residents of Woodbury; he was for several years
chairman of Hall county commision of roads and revenues, and
had been president of the Georgia State sanitarium; he is
survived by his wife, the former Miss Annie Perry, sister of
State Senator H. H. Perry, and two daughters, Misses Georgia
and Erskine Dixon; a member of the Methodist church, his
funeral was at his residence and interment was at Alta Vista
cemetery; [from Atlanta Constitution, no date stated] Vol. 31,
No. 10, February 6, 1903
MERIWETHER COUNTY, GA - NEWSPAPERS OBITS   Volume 31, December 5, 1902 - November
27, 1903

Dr. Dixon's daughter Erskine Dixon married Dr. John Rudolph in 1904. Their home, now 700
Green Street, was designed by Mrs. Rudolph and built by her mother Annie Perry Dixon. The
house, built in 1916, was known as the Dixon-Rudolph house. The house was home to Rudolph's
restaurant for many years.

Rock of Ages

Exodus 33:21-23

Then the LORD said, "There is a place near me where you may stand on a rock. When my glory passes by, I will put you in a cleft in the rock and cover you with my hand until I have passed by. Then I will remove my hand and you will see my back; but my face must not be seen."

Let Me Hide Myself in Thee

Rev. Walter Wangerin, Jr., author of *"The Rag Man"*, tells the gripping account of a man watching a Christ figure travel through his streets exchanging what is broken, sick and lost for hope and new life. When the witness of these things finds himself in the presence of the resurrected Christ he asks to be clothed, just as the others, with tired rags exchanging what was withered with the glorious and brilliant light of new life. It is a powerful story of transformation and salvation. It is our faith story if we will trust and share it.

Just as a drowning swimmer embraces an extended flotation device, we find a woman depicted clinging to the saving cross of Jesus Christ. The divine light that saves through all the storms and the foundation of strength that spans all the ages is the bedrock of her existence. Nothing else, no one else but God alone saves her. God alone is our salvation.

Two hundred and fifty years ago, Augustus Toplady, a Calvinist, wrote the words of the famous hymn, "Rock of Ages." So famous are his words that this hymn is celebrated as one of the top four hymns of the eighteenth century.

In the third verse of Toplady's hymn he describes that in recognizing our need for salvation we also see that we need to be clothed in Christ. The woman holding onto the cross is dressed only in her first layer of clothes, nearly naked. Her earthly and outward identity is cast away. The red robes have dropped away. She is both vulnerable and yet ready to be dressed.

The cleft of the rock is an image that Moses and Elijah share. The cleft is a safe haven and protection that is found in both the storm and the glory of God's presence. The image in the window reflects both in the same scene. The storm blows below as darkness surrounds and the mighty, divine light of judgment passes overhead. In both cases the cross keeps the faithful safe and secure.

173

The second and fourth stanzas offer an assurance that comes from holding fast to Jesus Christ. All our efforts to make ourselves new and whole cannot do what Christ has done for us. On the cross, we are made new and whole. It might take our entire lifetime to come to Christ, but even at our last breath Christ waits to heal and restore us. He offers the double cure: to make us whole and to love us.

The woman is not only holding onto the cross, she is also sharing the cross of Jesus. Her life is saved by the gift exchanged on the cross for us. Her eyes are focused on the Lord just as Peter had his eyes fixed on Jesus when he came walking on the water to be with Jesus in the storm.

The storms will come. Brokenness and separation will rage. We have nothing to bring but ourselves. In the waters of baptism we are claimed and through Christ's blood are our sins forgiven and our life made new. Fly to the cross and cling on tight!

Dr. John T. Brantley

In Memory of Carrie Finger. By Father & Brother.

"Rock of Ages" was written by the Rev. Augustus Montague Toplady in 1763. Toplady was traveling along the gorge of Burrington Combe in the Mendip Hills of England and was caught in a storm. He sought shelter in a crevice of rock and it was here that he was inspired with the title of the song.

Rock of Ages, cleft for me,
Let me hide myself in Thee;
Let the water and the blood,
From Thy wounded side which flowed,
Be of sin the double cure,
Save from wrath and make me pure.

Not the labor of my hands
Can fulfill Thy law's demands;
Could my zeal no respite know,
Could my tears forever flow,
All for sin could not atone;
Thou must save, and Thou alone.

Nothing in my hand I bring,
Simply to Thy cross I cling;
Naked, come to Thee for dress;
Helpless, look to Thee for grace;
Foul, I to the fountain fly;
Wash me, Savior, or I die.

While I draw this fleeting breath,
When my eyes shall close in death,
When I rise to worlds unknown,
And behold Thee on Thy throne,
Rock of Ages, cleft for me,
Let me hide myself in Thee.

Chapel-Right Side-Front to Back

The Angel and the Three Marys

Matthew 28 5-6

The angel said to the women, "Do not be afraid; for I know that you are looking for Jesus who has been crucified. He is not here, for He has risen, just as He said. Come, see the place where He was lying."

Mark 16:1

When the Sabbath was over, Mary Magdalene, and Mary the mother of James, and {Mary} Salome, bought spices, so that they might come and anoint Him.

HE IS RISEN, HE IS NOT HERE!

The angel's message to the disciples on the day of our Lord's resurrection, "He is risen, He is not here," has within it a truth and a mystery.

"He is risen" is the glorious reality that crowned the ministry of Jesus on earth. This statement is celebrated by Christians as the central truth of our faith. Without the actual and confirmed resurrection of Jesus Christ, our faith is lost in a history of good men who have done miraculous things. The resurrection event witnessed by those who were there and certified by centuries of Christians whose lives have been filled by his presence, make the angelic statement the most important truth ever uttered in the world.

"He is not here" is a statement that has within it the profound mystery that soon would be sounded around the world. He was not "there" as he had been. Now He was alive revealing himself to the eyes, heart and lives of the believers. "He is risen" quickly replaced the "He is not here" with the energy to change history forever. The claims of the "here" Jesus became the reality of the "everywhere" risen Christ.

On the walls of the Chapel of Gainesville First, persons who gather for study or worship view a display of stained glass windows which have inspired persons for nearly a century. The windows were brought from the downtown church when they made their transition to the lakeside. They remind persons of their historic local past, but more importantly they reflect the presence of the risen Christ. "He is risen, He is not here." Hallelujah!

Rev. Hugh Cauthen

In memory of
Dr. J. W. Oslin. Mrs. Annie E. Oslin.

On January 9, 1906, my precious father, Dr. J. W. Oslin, 'crossed over the river,' not a struggle, not a groan — grand ending of a grand life. I am so glad I saw him pass away; 'twas as peaceful, as gentle, as the rustle of an angel's wing' death will never seem so terrible again. I am glad, too, that I have such a beautiful memory of him as he lay in his casket; no trace of suffering, but youth, lingered there, and I could not realize that he would never awaken, so calm and grand he looked. / Words are empty in trying to portray his life! It was a 'living epistle known and read of all men' and the pages were fair and clean. Consistent, honest, true, tender and devoted in his family relations, courteous to everyone, he was a cultured, Christian gentleman, 'doing unto others as he would be done by.' How could his life be otherwise than beautiful, when the corner stone was Christian love, and that love embraced everyone, even his enemies; he had no enmity in his heart. Oh! we miss him so and will not see his like again soon.

His home life was ideal. Even the little children loved grandpa devotedly and were always willing to minister to him. He entertained them and advised them in such a kind, gentle way, and they felt that he loved them. His children and grandchildren will hang on memory's wall no picture more beautiful than the sweet, loving talks they had with him, and at times he would grow so poetical and eloquent, they would look up in wonder and delight.

Our counselor, champion, friend, — can it be that grand spirit is no more? and that his life is only a memory? No, he is not dead, but lives in our hearts and homes and is our father still and loves us tho' he has passed on the other side.

Father, we would not call thee back to suffering and pain but the sun does not shine so brightly nor do the birds sing as sweetly, yet we are trying hard to say 'Thy will be done' and take up life's burden again with a grand, sweet song. We know thou art at rest, dear father, but, there are aching hearts behind though we are assured of thy safety. He has often told me that he was not afraid to die but would meet death bravely when it came, and our faith will be strengthened and I trust our lives will be fashioned after a higher model since we saw him go — so calmly and peacefully; it is true that Jesus can make a dying bed 'as soft as downy pillows are.'

Then good-bye, father, though it tears the heart string to say it. Some sweet day with 'God's help, we'll bid you good morning in a fairer, brighter clime. Till then we must be content, for 'God's plans like lilies pure and white unfold.'

Mrs. J. W. Smith

Buried at Alta Vista, Gainesville GA.

(Dr. Olsin served in the Civil War as a surgeon for the 37 Alabama Regiment.)

Christ the Comforter

John 14:18,27

THE CHRIST OF COMFORT, arm outstretched in loving benediction as if to say to a broken, desolate, uncertain world populated with hurting hearts desperate for the reassurance of a counseling spirit: "I will not abandon you or leave you as orphans in the storm--I will come to you. I am leaving you with a gift--peace of mind and heart! And the peace I give isn't fragile like the peace the world gives. So don't be troubled or afraid." (John 14:18,27 The Living Bible) .

Rev. Jim Winn

Jesus Prays in Gethsemane

Matthew 26:36-39

Then Jesus went with his disciples to a place called Gethsemane, and he said to them, "Sit here while I go over there and pray." He took Peter and the two sons of Zebedee along with him, and he began to be sorrowful and troubled. Then he said to them, "My soul is overwhelmed with sorrow to the point of death. Stay here and keep watch with me."

Going a little farther, he fell with his face to the ground and prayed, "My Father, if it is possible, may this cup be taken from me. Yet not as I will, but as you will."

Prayer Life

The life of Jesus was one of unceasing prayer. After his baptism by John he went into the wilderness for a period of forty days where he prayed constantly. Prior to every event in his life Jesus prayed and sought the will of God. Immediately before his trial and crucifixion he went into the Garden of Gethsemane. In the garden he wrestled with the issue of His impending suffering. He would leave the garden with a sense of resoluteness about his fate.

Antonio Stradivari was the world's greatest violin maker. His instruments are unsurpassed in sweetness of tone. It has been a perplexing mystery to violin makers why this tone cannot be duplicated. The materials he used are available except for the formula for the varnish. The varnish enriches the tone and provides a soft luster instead of a shine. The formula for the finish is a mystery.

Jesus knew the formula for a vital relationship with God was not a secret; it was discovered through a vital prayer life. Prayer empowered and enabled Jesus to experience the humiliation, degradation, and suffering of Calvary.

The Reverend Jim Thompson knew the power of prayer and his life exhibited its attributes. His was a faith forged at the anvil of prayer and meditation. It was my privilege to serve with him in The North Georgia Cabinet. I constantly observed his faith and commitment to Christ and the Church. When he was confronted with a Garden of Gethsemane event he turned to faith to Christ who was his constant companion and strength.

L.B. Caywood

Senior Pastor 1990-1992

As his ministry unfolded, Jesus knew what God was asking of him, he knew what obedience would cost him and he knew what the outcome would be. He surrounded himself with his closest companions who wanted to be there for him, believed in him, were ready to fight for him but in the end betrayed him, denied him, and then deserted him. Matthew tells us that Jesus was 'sorrowful and troubled . . . overwhelmed with sorrow to the point of death'. Imagine the depth of the isolation that Jesus must have experienced in that time in the garden. His closest friends were right there, but were unable to comprehend what was happening to their Lord, they even fell asleep! Yet even in his darkest hour, Jesus turned to God in prayer and Matthew tells us that Jesus released everything to God the Father with the words, "Yet not as I will, but as you will." Jesus chose to do God's will so that you and I can have eternal life with him.

Has God ever asked you to face something that is so difficult that you question whether or not you have heard his request correctly? Have you ever tried to figure out a different way to do what God has asked you to do that is less risky, less painful, or tried to figure out who else is better qualified to do the task than you? When faced with difficult decisions, it is normal to seek help and advice from others, but when it comes down to the wire, when God has placed a call on your heart, you alone have to make choices and the final decision is yours alone. Do you go to him and answer "yes, your will be done?"

After volunteering for short-term mission work over several years, my husband and I felt we were being called into the long-term mission field. We prayed. We asked for insight from our pastor, our friends, and other missionaries in the field, and we prayed. What do we do now that we have made the decision to give up life as we have known it, left our families and friends behind, quit our jobs, sold our house, moved to a foreign country where we don't speak the language, and have begun a new life so that we can share the Gospel? We continue to turn, individually and together, to God in prayer. We don't have special insight into how our call will be lived out and we have many challenges ahead of us, but we do have faith in God who hears prayers and has promised to "be with you always, even to the end of the age" (Matthew 28:20b).

Jesus prayed throughout his ministry modeling a way to have an intimate, personal relationship with God, the Father. He invites each one of his children to know him intimately and call him Father. Do you share your innermost thoughts, concerns, desires, and yes, your fears with him? What will you say when God meets you in Gethsemane?

Karen and Michael Madsen

Prayer Logic

It is totally understandable that a logical and educated person would question the existence of God. The miracles described in the bible appear to be improbable and or impossible. If the actions attributed to God never happened then the whole thing seems to be a story created by man to control the actions of others. So what can the logical man do? Follow these instructions exactly. Find a quiet place and say the following. God, I do not know if you exist but if you do, I need your help. Will you please.........and then ask for what you want or need. Then say the Lord's Prayer. Then go back to life and do the best you can. In a few days and no more than a week later, repeat the process. Go back to life and try (and wait) and repeat every few days. One day you will feel the presence of God in your life. It will seem weird and you will not be sure. Notice I didn't say he would answer your prayer, but, you will feel his presence. Now you should go to your quiet place and say the following. God if what I felt was You, thank You. God, I do not know if you exist but if you do I need your help. Will you please.........and end with the Lord's Prayer. Continue to repeat every few days. With time you will see God's work in your life and if you keep your heart open and continue to pray one day you will be amazed at the miracles He has performed. Your prayers will change with time and become more frequent and eventually you will know Him and you will witness His power in your life. You will not just believe but you will know. When you know Him then questioning His existence is not an option.

It would not be logical.

Michael Tolson

Ham, H. W. J.

H. W. J. Ham Dead
In Gainesville, GA

Prominent Lecturer Expired
Yesterday After Brief
Illness

Gainesville, GA December 17 – H. W. J. Ham, known as "Snollygoster Ham, died
at his home at East Highlands last night at 12:35 o'clock, after, a four weeks'
illness. He was stricken with asthma and heart trouble in Chicago four weeks
ago while in a lecture tour and had two severe attacks on the train while
enroute home. It was necessary for him to cancel all engagements.

After arriving at home he grew better and was up yesterday. He was sitting up
when his heart stopped beating and he died.

Col. Ham was an ex-member of the legislature and had edited many newspapers.
He became famous as an orator and humorist during the early days of Populism in
Georgia and became known throughout the country for his fine humor and unique
expressions. After the campaign was over he was urged by many daily papers to
reduce his speeches to a lecture. He took the lecture platform and made a
magnificent success, being in demand throughout the nation.

But among those who knew him at home he was loved and admired for his beautiful
character, genial nature and many qualities. In the death of Colonel Ham, the
South has lost one of her most unique and picturesque figures. He was 56 years
of age.

Snollygoster: A shrewd unprincipled person, especially a politician. The term was popularized in the 1890's by
Georgia Democrat H.W. J. Ham throughout the country in the stump speech "The Snollygoster in Politics."

Chapel Narthex-Right Side

Ruth the Gleaner

Ruth 2:6-9

The overseer replied, "She is the Moabite who came back from Moab with Naomi. She said, 'Please let me glean and gather among the sheaves behind the harvesters.' She came into the field and has remained here from morning till now, except for a short rest in the shelter."

So Boaz said to Ruth, "My daughter, listen to me. Don't go and glean in another field and don't go away from here. Stay here with the women who work for me. Watch the field where the men are harvesting, and follow along after the women. I have told the men not to lay a hand on you. And whenever you are thirsty, go and get a drink from the water jars the men have filled."

Some fifty or so years ago I became interested in photography and bought an Olympic SLR camera. In my process of learning to use it, I started making pictures of different objects around town. One of the locations I chose was the stained glass windows from the inside the Sanctuary of the First Methodist Church on Green Street.

I went into the church Sanctuary on a Sunday afternoon when the rays of the sun were shining through the windows. When I saw this I was struck with the beauty and awesomeness of this sight. The thoughts in my mind went immediately to the song that says…"SURELY THE PRESENCE OF THE LORD IS IN THIS PLACE. I CAN SEE GOD'S MIGHTY POWER AND GOD'S GRACE."

With this awesome feeling I sought out one of the pictures that I recalled that was in reference to the pastor who was the pastor when the church was built, Rev. B.F. Fraser, who served from 1905 to 1908. It was a picture of Ruth in the gleaning fields and in the background looking on were Boaz and Naomi. Beneath the window was the inscription,"TO THE GLORY OF GOD IN LOVING MEMORY OF MRS. NANCY ISABELL GOODWIN MOTHER OF OUR BELOVED PASTOR, B.F. FRASER."

Another line of this song says, "IN THE MIDST OF HIS CHILDREN THE LORD SAID HE WOULD BE."

The Lord surely was with Rev. Fraser.

Willis McLemore

Rev. B. F. Fraser.

In many ways the pastor of the First Methodist Church in 1906, B.F. Fraser, was very similar to that of Rev. Jim Thompson in 1980. Both pastors had the difficult task of transitioning a congregation from an old and beloved Sanctuary to a new one. The following is an excerpt from "History of the First Methodist Church-1833-1906" written by J.C. Bickers.

Pastor's Preface

This work is gotten out not only as a piece of desirable local church and city history, but the proceeds of the sale are to be devoted to the "new church fund." Many sacred memories cluster about the old church-but infinitely more of inspiration and hope and life are manifest in the magnificent new structure now under way. Let the new temple be the expression of a newer faith, a bright hope, a firmer purpose of loyalty to the "Lamb's Bride."

On the splendid achievements of the past let us look for the greater victories in the future; from the struggles of the early church let us receive inspiration for sacrifice, and let every one of us have a part in the work.

Fraternally your pastor,

B.F. Fraser

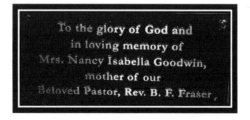

To the glory of God and
in loving memory of
Mrs. Nancy Isabella Goodwin,
mother of our
Beloved Pastor, Rev. B. F. Fraser

The B.F. in Rev. Fraser's name stands for Benjamin Franklin. At the time of this writing his granddaughter, Louise Cook, is a centenarian and resides in Gainesville at Lanier Village Estates. Mrs. Cook's father was B.F. Fraser Jr. and her brother B.F. Fraser III.

Chapel Narthex-Left Side

Jesus and The Beloved Disciple

John 13:23

There was reclining on Jesus' bosom one of His disciples, whom Jesus loved.

John

It has been established by scholars that John the son of Zebedee is the unnamed "beloved disciple" who occupies a prominent place in the Fourth Gospel that goes by his name.

At the last Supper he leans on the breast of Jesus, at the Cross he alone was faithful, and entrusted with the care of Jesus' mother, at the tomb was the first to believe in Jesus' Resurrection, and at the Sea of Galilee the first to recognize the Lord. Of the three inner circle of the Twelve, Peter, James, and John only John seems to fit the title of, "beloved disciple".

John was with Jesus in all of the important and dramatic moments of his life as recorded by the Gospels. Was he the favorite of Jesus? The Gospels do not intend it appears to me to be the case, but to show great devotion to Jesus on John's part.

In our world devotion to Jesus and the church often is seen in people and we often refer to those persons as the "salt of the earth" to quote Jesus, and in rare cases we say, "she\he is a saint". Those persons display an unusual amount of dedication, humility, and without desire for recognition. One out of the Twelve was singled out as "beloved", less than ten percent. That may be a few better points than we see in people today, but nevertheless there are those across history and today who qualify to be "beloved".

Hopefully this window in memory of Frank Wiegand, whom I remember as a "beloved" member of this congregation, will inspire more of us to become "beloved" in the service of our Lord.

Dr. Don Harp

Senior Minister 1983-1988

Given in Memory of
A. Frank Wiegand
by his friends and family
2003

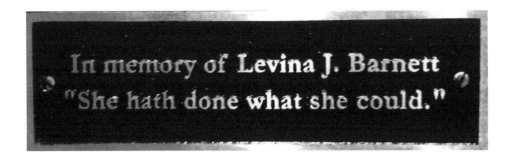

Mark 14:3-8

*And being in Bethany in the house of Simon the leper, as he sat at meat, there came a woman having an alabaster box of ointment of spikenard very precious; and she brake the box, and poured it on his head. And there were some that had indignation within themselves, and said, "Why was this waste of the ointment made? For it might have been sold for more than three hundred pence, and have been given to the poor?" And they murmured against her. And Jesus said, "Let her alone; why trouble ye her? She hath wrought a good work on me. For ye have the poor with you always, and whensoever ye will ye may do them good: but me ye have not always. **She hath done what she could**: she is come aforehand to anoint my body to the burying."*

The John the Beloved window in the Chapel Narthex has two plaques. The lower one is seen above and is the original inscription to this window. The "In Memory" portions of the Narthex windows were not used due to architectural constraints. If one is not familiar with this particular passage, you would think it was somewhat of an odd verse choice. It has almost an apologetic tone to it as if to say, "She did the best she could with what she had to work with" much like a coach explaining away a losing season or a child stating she could have made a better grade had she just studied more. As Rev. Phil DeMore was fond of saying in his sermons, "I wish it hadn't been said that way." However, on closer inspection the verse is perfect and the height of praise for a Christian. The unnamed woman in the Gospel of Mark is Mary of Bethany who is the sister of Martha and Lazarus. They are a family of means. The alabaster box is a vase made of a precious marble-like stone and the spikenard within an expensive fragrant perfume. One can imagine what Mary is feeling sitting in the presence of Jesus; the person who brought her brother back to life. Martha's preparations were necessary but Mary is compelled to do something exceptional; an act and a gift of love with no consideration of the cost. In anointing Jesus, symbolically, Mary gave all she could or in other words she gave something no one else could; she gave the **best** she had. She even endured the indignation of Judas, of all people, at the meal to honor Jesus. So this inscription portrays the ultimate compliment to Levina Barnett by her loved ones and most probably represents a testament to her having lived a pious and God filled life.

J.M.

Levina Barnett is not listed in the 1906 directory of members in J.C.Bickers' History of the Methodist Church.

Reception Hall-Center

The Reception Hall windows from the Green Street Church were given by the Gadabouts in 2002. Dot Strickland, a member of our church since the fifties, was instrumental in this endeavor. Legend has it that she and other members were playing cards in the Reception Hall and Dot remarked, "That is one big, ugly, plain wall. We should do something about that." Ada Florence Stovall quickly contributed the seed money and the rest is history.

Jesus Saves Peter

Matthew 14:30

But when he saw the wind, he was afraid and, beginning to sink, cried out,

"Lord, save me!"

Lord, Save Me!

22 Immediately Jesus made the disciples get into the boat and go on ahead of him to the other side, while he dismissed the crowd. 23 After he had dismissed them, he went up on a mountainside by himself to pray. Later that night, he was there alone, 24 and the boat was already a considerable distance from land, buffeted by the waves because the wind was against it.25 Shortly before dawn Jesus went out to them, walking on the lake. 26 When the disciples saw him walking on the lake, they were terrified. "It's a ghost," they said, and cried out in fear. 27 But Jesus immediately said to them: "Take courage! It is I. Don't be afraid."28 "Lord, if it's you," Peter replied, "tell me to come to you on the water."29 "Come," he said. Then Peter got down out of the boat, walked on the water and came toward Jesus. 30 But when he saw the wind, he was afraid and, beginning to sink, cried out, "Lord, save me!" 31 Immediately Jesus reached out his hand and caught him. "You of little faith," he said, "why did you doubt?"32 And when they climbed into the boat, the wind died down. 33 Then those who were in the boat worshiped him, saying, "Truly you are the Son of God."34 When they had crossed over, they landed at Gennesaret. 35 And when the men of that place recognized Jesus, they sent word to all the surrounding country. People brought all their sick to him 36 and begged him to let the sick just touch the edge of his cloak, and all who touched it were healed. Matthew 14:22-36 NIV

Peter's is a character full of enthusiasm and passion. How many of us can relate to his devotion to God and his impulsive response to Christ's call? Peter and his brother answered the call from Jesus, "Come, follow me and I will send you out to fish for people." (Matthew 4:19 NIV) It doesn't say Peter thought about it, wrote his parents for counsel, or made a pros and cons list. Jesus Christ called him, and he followed. Scripture tells us, "At once they left their nets and followed him." (Matthew 4:20 NIV). At once. Immediately.

After following Christ and serving in his ministry, Peter had witnessed many miracles. He longed to be in Christ's presence. After one session of preaching and healing, Christ took time to rejuvenate. He went up the mountainside to pray alone. Later, when Jesus was ready to continue to serve he started out across the turbulent water to rejoin his disciples. Though they had just spent time with Him, knew that He was Lord, the disciples were immediately skeptical and frightened to see Jesus walking on water. Not, Peter! He was ready to jump in and join Christ wherever or however necessary. Peter asked Jesus to invite him onto the water. As he started walking, Peter looked out to the waves and doubted. His fear immediately caused him to falter and sink. How often do we get excited about being with Christ, only to sink with doubt and fear when the waves of life wash up around us?

Peter reminds us that all we have to do is call out to Jesus in our time of need.

"Lord, save me!"

Prayer

Lord, Jesus, thank you for loving us for who we are; whether enthusiastic and passionate or doubtful and fearful. You know our hearts, Lord. We praise You and Your miraculous power. We want to follow you. Guide us through our doubt and fears back to You. Thank you for reaching out to us and pulling us back in the boat, when we are in over our heads. Thank you for coming to our aide when we cry for help. Lord, save us! Amen

Lisa Bisson

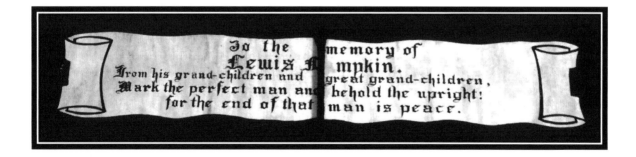

Reception Hall-Left

Christ and the Woman of Samaria at the Well.

John 4:4-8

Now he had to go through Samaria. So he came to a town in Samaria called Sychar, near the plot of ground Jacob had given to his son Joseph. Jacob's well was there, and Jesus, tired as he was from the journey, sat down by the well. It was about noon.

When a Samaritan woman came to draw water, Jesus said to her, "Will you give me a drink?" (His disciples had gone into the town to buy food.)

Jesus knew what the needs and heart's desires were of the woman at the well. We are given some of the circumstances of her life, not to judge or condemn her, but to identify with her. She already knew what her failures were, so I don't think Jesus was reminding her of her dismal marital circumstances or the fallacies of her beliefs to reprimand her, but to open her eyes to just what her "thirst" was really for.

Since she came to the well in the heat of the day, she already knew that she was a social outcast among the women. Her arriving at the well at noon showed that she was only doing what we so often do when we avoid certain circumstances and certain people because it is too painful to bear the condemning looks and whispers behind backs. Because of her defensive responses to Jesus, she demonstrated that she knew the Jews looked down on her and her beliefs.

Is it a loving, Jesus-like response for us to talk about her low morals and behaviors? Or, is it a more "kingdom of God" oriented response to recognize our own failures and shortcomings in her story and offer a more kind and understanding heart to the "women at the well" in our world?

We all try to satisfy our own thirst for whatever our need is before we come to realize that nothing we can accomplish or acquire in the way of worldly status, relationships, or material possessions will fulfill our deepest hearts' desires. Only when we recognize who Jesus is and what he has done for us can we recognize what love and acceptance feel like. And only when we realize that any true freedom we have is from total surrender to God will we be able to live out our daily lives loving and serving others just as Jesus, the Christ, loved and served those on earth he came in contact with.

Prayer:

Dear Heavenly Father,

Thank you for your gift of living water. Give us the capacity to see other's circumstances as opportunities to love and serve them by sharing your grace, love and mercy, so that they, too, will experience your kingdom come.

In Jesus' name,
Amen

Joyce Link

In memory of Indianor Palmour. 1854. 1907.

Resurrected Jesus-Touch Me Not

DO NOT HOLD ON TO ME

John 20:15-17

Jesus said to her, "Woman, why are you weeping? Whom are you looking for?" Supposing him to be the gardener, she said to him, "Sir, if you have carried him away, tell me where you have laid him, and I will take him away." Jesus said to her, "Mary!" She turned and said to him in Hebrew, "Rabbouni!" (which means Teacher). Jesus said to her, "Do not hold on to me, because I have not yet ascended to the Father. But go to my brothers and say to them, 'I am ascending to my Father and your Father, to my God and your God.'"

The story that inspired this window comes from the first Easter, when Mary Magdalene has just discovered the stone rolled away from the tomb. She ran to John and Peter who joined her at the tomb. In her grief, she stood outside weeping. Then, she encountered Jesus. The text implies that Mary hugged him, but Jesus surprised Mary and us when he said to Mary "Do not hold on to me." Why would Jesus tell Mary "Do not hold on to me?" This is the Messiah who welcomed all, who invited children to come to him, whose healing hands touched those whom no one else dared to touch, who challenged Thomas to place his hand in the side of Jesus. Now Jesus, on the Day of Resurrection, says to beloved Mary, "Do not hold on to me." It seems baffling, but the answer is in the language. The Greek word for hold implies clinging, holding back, restraining. Thus Jesus says to Mary, "Do not restrain me, because I have not yet ascended." Jesus tells Mary that she cannot hold this moment, because God's work is not complete.

In times of great emotion, human nature recoils. We want to stop. We want to hold on to the moment. Whether our emotion be grief or joy or sorrow, we want to preserve what is rather than consider what might be. The reason we cling so closely to the status quo is fear. We fear that things might get worse or that we might lose a joyful moment. The scripture tells us that perfect faith casts out fear, because faith is always willing to trust God for every tomorrow. In the midst of sorrow or worry, by faith, we believe that God will lead us to a better tomorrow. In the midst of joy, we can experience it fully, not trying to preserve it, because by faith we believe that God has many more days of joy ahead.

Mary, grieving Jesus' cruel death, held on to him in the moment. Unaware of the glory that had yet to be revealed, she clung closely to Jesus. In effect Jesus said "Don't cling to this moment. There are better things ahead." His invitation is to faith. Can you dare to believe that there are better things ahead? Can you trust that tomorrow holds more than what you can see?

This stained glass window stands in the reception hall, posing the question to all who enter this sacred space: do you have faith to believe that tomorrow holds more than you can see? For those who answer yes, there is always hope.

Dr. Glenn Ethridge

The Bickers family has a prominent place in the history of the First Methodist Church. The book, "History of the First Methodist Church", was written by J.C. Bickers who was the son of Garnett and Martha Bickers. In that book it is noted that Garnett Bickers was one of the early presidents of the Epworth League (an organization of the young life of the church) which was established in 1892. Mrs. Bickers was active in the early church as well and served as lady manager of The Juvenile Missionary Society which was organized in 1885. She also served as lady manager of the Junior Epworth League organized in 1896 until it was merged with the Senior League.

In J.C. Bickers' book Bessie Bickers is listed as a daughter of Garnett and Martha Bickers. Bessie Bickers was a Hall County school teacher and founded, in 1913, one of the first Humane Societies in Georgia. Known as Miss Bessie, she held one adopting an animal to the same standards as if they were adopting a child. The Hall County Humane Society still recognizes the importance of her contributions and anyone adopting an animal today must sign "Miss Bessie's Pledge."

Miss Bessie Bickers, December 15, 1972. Photograph of Miss Bessie Bickers, shown with some of her animals and youthful animal lovers. "Miss Bessie" was honored on December 15, 1972, by the First Federal Savings & Loan Association of Gainesville as "First Citizen" for that year. She served for many years as Executive Director of the Hall County Humane Society, located on Ridge Road.

Girl Pointing to the Fifth Commandment

"Honor Thy Father and Mother"

Exodus 20:12

"Honor your father and your mother, so that you may live long in the land the LORD your God is giving you."

This window is currently in storage for later use. This picture was taken by Willis McLemore in the early 1960's as part of a class he was taking on photography. This window's inscription is "Epworth League 1908."The interpretation is from Henry Willet's "Report on the Old Windows." He surmised that the girl was probably a daughter of the donor.

Pointing Out What's Hidden

I'm my parent's child. I was named after my father and I took the skin complexion of my mother. My father stood 5'11 and my mother 4'11. I'm 5'5''. Daddy was a concrete finisher with a 3rd grade education. Mama graduated with an 11th grade education and retired from the Wrigley Company. Both pointed out the hidden value of hard work and the importance of education.

I remember showing my 3rd grade report card to my parents. Daddy looked at the card and retorted, "Son, keep up the good work. You can't beat education." Mama was a harder sale. She smiled at my card, saying that she was proud of me for A's in all of the subjects except for one. She pointed to the class that I received a B and asked me "Where's the 'A?'" She knew that I could do better. From that day forward, I was committed to making all A's to honor my parents. And when I didn't quite make it, they always asked if I did my best and would celebrate a B- or C just as much as they celebrated the A.

These early experiences shaped me into the person I am today. Though hidden my awareness at the time, my parent's were laying a foundation for me to build upon. A foundation that I've chosen to build a life that honors them both.

Today it's become more challenging for parents and children to follow the script my parents provided for me. There's a lot more things competing for our children's attention and loyalty that challenges the relationship between parents and children.

In the days the Bible was being written, God blessed people who took care of their parents. The people of God lived in community where there wasn't a home for the elderly. Parents took care of their kids, and eventually kids would take care of their parents. Everyone helped everyone as was required by the Ten Commandments.

The second tablet of the Ten Commandment begins with the command to "Honor your father and mother…" There were two tablets that divided ways to approach our relationship with God (the first tablet that includes commandments 1-4) and ways to approach our relationships with one another (commandments 5-10).

A lesser-known stain glass window from the old church is hidden from sight. It remains in a plywood box incased in a wall and shows a little girl pointing to the Fifth Commandment. When thinking about the little girl pointing to the commandment, I wondered what her challenges were to honor her parents. I also got curious as to why it is a little girl and not a little boy. But there were two questions that I continued to wrestle with that I couldn't shake: "What remains hidden from sight in the 5th commandment today?" and "What does it mean for us to point to the 5th Commandment?"

One of the things that remain hidden from our memories is the story behind the Commandments. Before they were enslaved in Egypt, the Hebrews people were not a nation, but a collection of nomadic families. Tribal leaders who didn't always act honorably led these families. From time to time, the leaders would squabble over grazing rights of animals and some were guilty of raiding each other's camps to steal flocks and herds. But all of this changed with the giving of the Ten Commandments at Mount Sinai.

During their wanderings in the wilderness en route to the Promised Land, the Hebrew people developed a vision of nation-hood and a settled life. Once they were established in the Promised Land, they ceased to be nomadic herdsmen, and became farmers, within designated areas. It was no longer enough for each male to be a tribal leader, priest, lawgiver and policeman to his own, immediate family or group. Something greater and yet hidden from their awareness was emerging: a changing society that required a far wider form of governance to oversee the families, clans, and tribes that were becoming a settled nation.

Now being attached to the developing concept of "family life" went far beyond local relatives and dependents, and included all those who claimed descent from Abraham. A new sense of family life made them recognize the corporate and spiritual nature of their calling to be God's people. Their small, local family units, that epitomized honoring one's physical father and mother was merely the starting point and not the end. Each small, family group was part of the greater whole—part of being included in God's family.

It's an honor to be part of God's family. The Hebrew word for "honor" literally means to "be heavy," or "weighty." Today we say that a person's words "carry a lot of weight." During the loss of a loved one, we often hear the words, "Our hearts are 'heavy.'" Someone whose words are weighty or who makes our hearts heavy is a person worthy of honor and respect.

So when God commands us to honor our parents, God is telling us that our parents are worthy of high value and respect. Admittedly, for many people, however, it is increasingly difficult to honor their parents—at least ways we have been taught—who don't act honorably towards their children. We need a prayerful and supportive community to help us learn to forgive our parents for being humans, while not letting them off of the hook if they violated us.

Forgiveness helps us to accept that our parents are the way they are and that they may never change. Surprisingly, the hidden truth behind the act of forgiveness actually honors them as people: They have the right to be everything they want to be, you just don't have to stick around for their choices anymore.

So what does it mean for us to point to the 5th Commandment? Perhaps it simply means to honor the people (whether biological or not) who took care of us, nurtured us, protected us, loved us, and still love us. For young children, this means obeying parents. For teenagers, it suggests showing respect for Mom and Dad even if you *think* you know more than they do. For young adults, it means including your parents in your life—and not just remembering them on Mother's and Father's Day. For those in middle age and beyond, it means making sure that our parents are cared for as they move into old age or their health declines. And finally, for people like myself, whose parents have passed away, it means making your parents proud, since in many ways we point the way to their legacies.

Quincy D. Brown

Associate Minister (1995-1997)

The Easter Lily-The White Robed Apostle of Hope

Symbol of purity, the resurrection of Jesus and the hope of life everlasting.

This stained glass window is above the front doors of the Old Green Steet Methodist Church.

Door Lights of Narthex and Sanctuary

Narthex

Angels of Praise and Acts of Mercy

Far Left Narthex Door Light

Angel of Praise with Censer

Center Narthex Door Lights

Left- Loaves of Bread

Right- Lamp Shining Brightly

Far Right Narthex Door Light

Angel of Praise and Trumpet

Sanctuary

Old Testament Doors (courtyard)

Left Door Light

Noah and the Ark

Right Door Light

The Good Shepherd

Right Altar Door Light/Left Altar Door Light

Joy, Variety and Color of Creation

As Described in the Psalms

Narthex Far Left Door Light

Angel of Praise with a Censer

The Censer

Leviticus 16:12

He is to take a censer full of burning coals from the altar before the LORD and two handfuls of finely ground fragrant incense and take them behind the curtain.

Psalm 141:1-2

I call to you, LORD, come quickly to me;
hear me when I call to you.
May my prayer be set before you like incense;
may the lifting up of my hands be like the evening sacrifice.

Revelation 5:8

And when he had taken it, the four living creatures and the twenty-four elders fell down before the Lamb. Each one had a harp and they were holding golden bowls full of incense, which are the prayers of God's people.

Revelation 8:3-5

Another angel, who had a golden censer, came and stood at the altar. He was given much incense to offer, with the prayers of all God's people, on the golden altar in front of the throne. The smoke of the incense, together with the prayers of God's people, went up before God from the angel's hand. Then the angel took the censer, filled it with fire from the altar, and hurled it on the earth; and there came peals of thunder, rumblings, flashes of lightning and an earthquake.

The censer is a container, usually with a closed top, containing hot charcoal that is used to burn incense. (Incense is derived from the Latin word *incensum* or to set on fire.) Frankincense and myrrh are common substances used for incense because of the strong and aromatic smoke produced when they burn. The smoke of burning incense is interpreted as a symbol of the prayer of the faithful rising to heaven and symbolic of giving a pleasing sacrifice to the Lord.

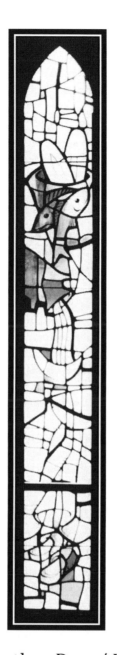

Center Narthex Door/ Left Light

Basket of Loaves and Two Fish

Water Pouring into Cup

The Serape(blanketlike shawl) and Sandals

Left Door Light Symbolism

Top to Bottom

Matthew 14:19-21

And he directed the people to sit down on the grass. Taking the five loaves and the two fish and looking up to heaven, he gave thanks and broke the loaves. Then he gave them to the people. They all ate and were satisfied, and the disciples picked up twelve basketfuls of broken pieces that were left over. The number of those who ate was about five thousand men, besides women and children.

Basket of loaves and two fish not only to recall the feeding of the multitude, but to remind us to feed our hungry brothers and sisters.

Water poured from a jug into a cup emphasizes giving drink to the thirsty. The window also reminds us to consider and use water as one of our precious gifts.

The serape and the sandals tell us to clothe the naked and to be aware of how others often live without the necessities of life.

Center Narthex Door /Right Light

Lamp Shining Brightly

Olive Branchs/Flagon Pouring Oil

Small Room and Candle on a Table

Prison Door with Key

Right Door Light Symbolism

Top to Bottom

Matthew 7:15-20

"Beware of false prophets, who come to you in sheep's clothing, but inwardly they are ravenous wolves. You will know them by their fruits. Do men gather grapes from thorn bushes or figs from thistles? Even so, every good tree bears good fruit, but a bad tree bears bad fruit. A good tree cannot bear bad fruit, nor can a bad tree bear good fruit. Every tree that does not bear good fruit is cut down and thrown into the fire. Therefore by their fruits you will know them."

A lamp shining brightly signifies the soul alive with grace and charity.

Olive branches and a small flagon pouring oil are both symbols of healing. Roses are represented to emphasize the sweet unction of visiting and comforting the sick.

A small room is seen at the bottom with a table upon which a candle burns smybolizing hospitality in welcoming of the stranger and the homeless, for in doing so, we welcome Christ Himself.

A prison door with a key invites us to visit the "imprisoned" both in the literal and figurative sense of the word.

"By their fruits you will know them."

Narthex

Far Right Door Light

Angel of Praise and Trumpet

211

The Trumpet

Numbers 10:1-7

The L<small>ORD</small> said to Moses: "Make two trumpets of hammered silver, and use them for calling the community together and for having the camps set out. When both are sounded, the whole community is to assemble before you at the entrance to the tent of meeting. If only one is sounded, the leaders—the heads of the clans of Israel—are to assemble before you. When a trumpet blast is sounded, the tribes camping on the east are to set out. At the sounding of a second blast, the camps on the south are to set out. The blast will be the signal for setting out. To gather the assembly, blow the trumpets, but not with the signal for setting out.

Joshua 6:4-5

Have seven priests carry trumpets of rams' horns in front of the ark. On the seventh day, march around the city seven times, with the priests blowing the trumpets. When you hear them sound a long blast on the trumpets, have the whole army give a loud shout; then the wall of the city will collapse and the army will go up, everyone straight in."

Matthew 24:31

And he will send his angels with a loud trumpet call, and they will gather his elect from the four winds, from one end of the heavens to the other.

Revelation 8:2

And I saw the seven angels who stand before God, and seven trumpets were given to them.

Revelation 11:15

The seventh angel sounded his trumpet, and there were loud voices in heaven, which said: "The kingdom of the world has become the kingdom of our Lord and of his Messiah, and he will reign forever and ever."

Sanctuary

Old Testament Side

Right Door Light

The Good Shepherd and His Sheep

213

Psalm 23

My shepherd is the Lord; there is nothing I shall want.

The Good Shepherd is represented lovingly tending his sheep. One is carried on his shoulder and another stands at his feet.

The Narthex and Sancturay door lights were placed several years after the large Sanctuary windows. The Sancutary windows form figures by the arrangement of various shapes of colored glass and is a charactristic technique of the Willet Stained Glass Studios. Willet also did the door lights, however as seen above , the colored glass is painted. This has added detail and was probably necessary because of the limited space of the narrow door lights. In this respect the door lights are very similar to the old windows in the Chapel and Reception hall.

Sanctuary

Old Testament Side

Left Door Light

Noah's Ark

Noah and the Ark

Genesis 8:11

The dove returned to him in the evening, but in its beak there was an olive leaf that it had plucked! So Noah knew that the flood waters had decreased on the land.

Depicted in this door light is Noah on the deck of the ark waiting for the return of the dove with the olive branch. You see at the top the dove and branch, in the middle the Ark and a fish with waves of the ocean at the bottom.

Sanctuary

Right Altar Door Light

Joy, Variety, and Color of Creation

Psalms: 96,145,147,148.

Door Lights to the Right and Left of the Altar

The two door lights on each side of the altar are meant to suggest the joy, infinite variety, and color found throughout creation as praised by the psalmist.

Psalm 96: *Oh sing to the Lord a new song all the earth. Declare his glory among nations.*

Psalm 145: *All your works shall give thanks to You, O Lord, and all your faithful shall bless you.*

Psalm 147: *Make melody to god on the lyre, He covers the heavens with clouds, Prepares rain for the earth. He makes his wind blow and the waters flow.*

Psalm 148: *Praise the Lord from the earth, you sea monsters and all deeps, Fire and hail, snow and frost, Mountains and all hills, fruit trees and all cedars, Wild animals and all cattle, Creeping things and flying birds...*

The left door light specifically shows radiant light spilling from the top of the window. Warm flower and fruit-like blossoms signifying the generativity of God's creative love and the fruits of the earth. The deep blue green at the bottom symbolizes water which nourishes all of life.

Sanctuary

Left Altar Door Light

Radiant Light/Flower and Fruit

Water That Nourishes All of Life

Memorable quotes found in the correspondence between the principals during the construction of the windows.

April 11, 1978

E. Crosby Willet to Reverend James Thompson (Stained glass window proposal)

"The windows will be a major influence on the final success of the building as they will create the mood needed for a suitable sanctuary for worship."

"I believe faceted glass will work well in this area. The epoxy matrix will give almost a stone like effect, filigree that will go well with the gothic forms of the wood surrounds."

"I feel it will also be a wonderful place to remind the worshipper through symbolism and figures woven through the design of the great truths of our religion."

"I'll be glad to develop my ideas for themes more completely and work out a lumiere design. Having a design in color is a wonderful sales tool for donors. Let me know and I'll get to work on it immediately."

January 9, 1979

E. Crosby Willet to Reverend James Thompson

"It was good to talk to you on Wednesday and I am glad that there is good progress on your church. My dad and I will be in your area during late February or March and will welcome an opportunity to discuss the windows. Best wishes for a wonderful 1979."

June 4, 1979

Henry Willet to James Barker

"I had the most inspiring visit to your new church with Pastor Thompson just at the moment when the first of the soaring arches had been erected. We were able to visualize what the opportunities were for creating outstanding windows suitable to your architectural concept, scale, light conditions, and relationship to iconography. In other words it was mighty exciting!"

August 15, 1979

James Barker to Henry Willet

"We have heard that you have been in touch with the contractor asking for shop drawings and suggesting changes in the window framing. May we request that all future correspondence and communication be direct through this office in order to avoid mistakes such as were made by your firm in The Northside Drive Baptist Church."

"Time is running out and we much make decisions soon. Now that the building up and the roof on, it is Ingrid's feeling and mine that we should definitely consider other concepts along with faceted glass. Since this is a window within a window, we feel the bronze glass should come sweeping through it to prevent the window from appearing that the church ran out of money and could not finish the great glass walls."

October 11, 1979

Henry Willet to James Barker

"The plan for the church you have is not only outstanding, but so very original and I think you will agree it calls for creating truly original and artistic stained glass that will sensitize with the architecture."

"The leading (for the stained glass) is not just for holding pieces of glass together, but hand-crafted in varying widths to accomplish a most effective treatment. I get so excited just envisioning it."

"I hope your daughter (Ingrid Barker-daughter of James Barker and one of the first women in America to have a degree in Architectural Iconography) will be available. I want to work out with her about coming up and visiting us and seeing how the studio works and meeting the staff. We have fifty very dedicated associates she will enjoy getting to know."

November 13, 1979

Henry Willet to Reverend James Thompson

"Sorry I can't meet with the committee with slides demonstrating the differences in quality. You and the architect are knowledgeable, but the average layman finds it hard to account for the differences in price. For instance, you could take our design and glass it all up in quarter inch lead then paint the artistically varying widths of the leading on the glass for a pseudo-effect. This would probably cost 15-20% less. There are lots of ways to cut cost, selecting cheaper glass, etc. We are figuring on an outstanding job-the finest in character with the architecture."

"Dean Sayre said there were only three authentic Episcopal Cathedrals in the U.S.A. Washington Cathedral, St. John the Devine, N.Y.C., and Grace Cathedral, San Francisco. We are the only studio that has been commissioned to do windows in all three. In other words, I feel we can truly create for you the finest in glass for the individual opportunity and challenge your church offers. We would collaborate very closely with you, your committee and architects to accomplish this."

November 21, 1979

Henry Willet to Reverend James Thompson

"It was such a joy to get the good news. (Willet studios awarded the stained glass windows contract) It will be a great challenge. Crosby and I and all the "gang" at the studio are appreciative of this great opportunity. I believe Ms. Barker will drive me up to Gainesville which will be fine."

221

November 27, 1979

Henry Willet to Reverend Thompson on being awarded the contract for the windows

"All Willet stained glass windows are fabricated of the finest glasses, both imported and domestic, with the choicest mouth-blown pot-metal glasses and Norman slabs to be used. All painted glasses will be fused in a kiln a sufficient number of times to render them fadeless as the work of the medieval glass artists which has stood the test of centuries."

February 19, 1980

Reverend James Thompson to Henry Willet

"I telephoned Crosby yesterday to tell him we wanted to switch arches. Instead of doing the right arch on the west elevation, we would like to do the left arch that includes the nativity, baptism of Jesus, and the calling of the twelve. As we discussed her in the office yesterday, I also would like for you to strengthen the right section of that window both by using some gold colors etc., and also by making the symbols in the window stand out a bit more. We also discussed the fact that the kite (The Phoenix) needs to be strengthened. In addition, we would like the have a touch of blue in the left section if possible."

February 26, 1980

Reverend James Thompson to Henry Willet

"On the center panel of the west elevation (lake side), we would like for you to make chalice more prominent and the phoenix more discernible and a bit more "phoenix-like" rather than "dove like.""

"As far as the entry is concerned, we would like Pentecost to be the prominent feature along with the conversion of Paul, the preaching of Peter or the vision of Peter (Acts 10: 9-16) and the conversion of Cornelius. Other minor themes might be the stoning of Stephen and the shipwreck of Paul. We do want Peter and Paul to have prominence in the windows and equally so."

"Other people we would like to portray would be Augustine, Luther, Calvin and particularly John and Charles Wesley and Frances Asbury. This may be too much for that area so if you have to leave someone out – don't let it be Wesley. Knowing you, you would leave out Wesley and put Calvin in!" (Henry Willet was very active in the Presbyterian Church in Philadelphia.)

"I am still working and praying on the last of the panels."

May 3, 1980

Henry Willet to Reverend James Thompson

"To date we have not received back the lumiere on the large entrance transom which we need. It is very exciting that we are working on the big window. Ingrid Barker has been here this week for "indoctrination.""

222

May 21, 1980

Ingrid Barker to Willet Stained Glass Studios

"To the designers, craftsman, workers, employees, the crew, and various people on the side (did I forget anyone!?) with Willet Studios- I want to send my enormous thanks for welcoming me to Philadelphia and the studio. I can't tell you how much I enjoyed myself and how much I learned by just observing the various processes of putting a window together. I really appreciated all the time everyone took with me- And I must say I was pleased as punch to find Philadelphians so cordial, warm, and friendly. Please keep up the good work and I hope that I will be able to come back soon"

May 1980

Ingrid Barker to Henry Willet

"Now that I've found a few moments of time, a proper thank you note is in order (Here it is!). My work was, as usual, in pure chaos when I got back and I thought I would never get through the mess last week. Somehow, I did. Gainesville has a wedding scheduled for June 25- and will have their first services in the sanctuary June 29. Is it possible to have any windows by then? They aren't expecting any. Business aside, I can't tell you how much I enjoyed my stay. Everyone was so nice and wonderful (including you, too!) I also wasn't expecting a crisp bill on the train, either. What a surprise! (You really didn't have to do that, you). The trip meant a lot to me, too."

July 1, 1980

Henry Willet to James Barker

"Sorry to miss you at Gainesville on Monday. I didn't arrive downtown until 1 P.M. The Church is really exciting as it approaches completion. All it needs is its "crowning glory", the stained glass. The East window and the transoms I expect will be installed the end of August. The lumiere for the West window I left with Jim Thompson. He was very pleased except he wanted the "horns" eliminated from Moses (too bad) and the mammoth locust, which I told Charlie Lawrence was way out of scale, (good criticism)."

August 4, 1980

Excerpt of report on existing stained glass in Old First Methodist Church Gainesville

"Enclosed is my report on the old windows. Sorry it couldn't have been more inviting. The older members would probably shoot me at speaking so disparagingly about their beloved windows."

"The ornamental work is of no great value or artistic interest. In fact, the windows, honestly speaking , would not be bought for artistic merit or value. The main value would be for a church that had no windows and couldn't afford new windows. The subjects have been largely taken from German religious painters of that era. Naturally the windows could have a strong nostalgic attraction for the former members of the church."

223

Respectfully submitted,

Henry Lee Willet, D.F.A.

Reverend James Thompson to Henry Willet

September 16, 1980

"The sanctuary windows are magnificent an almost breath-taking to behold. The lancets on each side of the doors are also good-except that you kept Calvin's coat of arms. Shame on you."

"But...the arches over the doors leave a great deal to be desired. In fact, they do not look as if they were a part of the same series as those in the sanctuary. The tongues of fire in the Pentecost window are not vivid enough to be able to tell what they are, and there is still that long strip of no color in that same panel that I asked you to correct. In all three of these windows there is too distinct a border of clear glass that just does not look good. The general effect of the three arches is pale and somewhat washed out in contrast to the beautiful windows in the sanctuary. I also pointed this out when you came down to bring us the lumiere. Something must be done!"

"I have paid the full amount to Tom, but I am counting on you to get these three arches in the narthex up to par with your other work."

Report on Stained Glass Windows to Dr. James Thompson

By Henry Willet

September 1980

When I entered the Church I put out of my mind everything I knew, heard or surmised. I approached the interior with only the thought I had, you had, the architects had, what we dreamed and hoped would be created.

The total concept I found breathtaking. Without a doubt, I feel pleased that the glass has accomplished its main purpose, to create a liturgical atmosphere to the greater glory of God.

As Henry Adams says in Mont Saint Michael and Chartres, the first command of the Queen of Heaven is for light and second and equally important, is color. Yes, we have color but the light and open effect has been maintained. We had two other commands which I feel have been followed most successfully.

One was to synchronize these three soaring arches into the wall of practically clear glass which has been accomplished by weaving some of the surrounding glass into the leaded stained glass.

Over and over again it was stressed, "We don't want to lose contact with the outdoors." I feel because as either flanking end we have enough clear glass so that the outside is completely discernible, an abrupt ending of the exterior view when it meets the leaded stained glass is thus eliminated.

The color selection is exciting without being garish. The leaded stained glass truly sings joyously.

As to the iconography, we wanted the window to communicate the wonderful message of our faith but subtlely.

The worst "compliment" that can be expressed about stained glass windows is, "My isn't that a perfect picture of Christ knocking at the door. It looks just like the Holman Hunt painting. What perspective! Look at the blue in Christ's eyes, etc., etc., etc.!"

A stained glass window is the handmaiden of architecture. It must be treated as a part of the wall surface. It must be kept two dimensional, flat and decorative.

A window is to be an aid to worship, not an idol or be worshipped. Like the Bible itself, a window has been read and re-read and then different and unexpected truths and incidents are discovered as the worshipper comes back time and time again. Start reading the Gospel of St. John. It moves you and stirs you but it takes many readings and much study to reveal the whole message. The same is true of a window.

I personally feel we have created stained glass that is both glorious in the best experience of the cardinal principle of our medium and a completely fresh and original concept.

Having enjoyed the windows for over an hour, I then took over thirty pictures (slides) of the windows in toto, in parts and many close-up details. The brought me down to an analytical approach to all the details.

I studied carefully the questions that had been raised and critically studied what I thought was wrong or could be improved. In the sanctuary the flanking windows were above reproach. Just great! At first my only thought was that were possibly was too much of the pure white in the dove in the Baptism scene but on further study and when Jim Cantrell came along and told me had two sections of the window that particularly inspired him, it turned out this dove section was one of the two. Then I restudied it and realized that it really fitted in place and created the expression needed.

I don't agree with the thought that the phoenix doesn't read out plainly enough. I find it very perky-soaring with great haste to get away from the hot flames and ashes. I have studied it carefully and also with the lumieres and can't suggest how it could be made more obvious keeping it in the context with the rest of the window.

I agree that the two small pieces above Our Lord's uplifted right hand would be more symbolic in a burgundy-purple color.

As to the Narthex, I was greatly relieved about the misunderstanding when I found the color palette of the transom windows and the sanctuary windows are the same when there is an even light like I had.

If you stand in the center aisle by the third pew from the back of the Gospel side and look at the Narthex windows, you will see both the Narthex window and the sanctuary window reflected in the Narthex screen and see that, if anything, the coloring in the Narthex is slightly darker due to the overhang.

We tried to keep the upper part of the Narthex lighter because they are viewed against the dark ceiling of the overhang while the lower parts are viewed against the light color of the side walls.

With all the crisscrossing arches there is confusion, but there is nothing that can be done about it.

The shield at the top of the right panel is John Wesley's. The word "Hark" and the music refer to Charles Wesley, the hymn writer. At the bottom are Asbury on horseback and an open Bible. On the left are Augustine of Hippo, Luther, and Calvin's heart and hand at the bottom.

We knew we had to keep the Narthex as light as possible since the need there is a different from the sanctuary. These were designed lighter and have adhered to the specifications as planned. I am sure you will find the lighter glasses in the perimeter are proper. What annoyed me were the heavy pieces of olive that should have been light colors like the rest of the perimeter glass and I think it would be an improvement if the Pentecostal flames were more ruby. While the figure in white, to the right of Peter is exactly as it was designed in the lumiere, if it were more of a purple color so it doesn't sink into the background, it would make a big change in the bringing the central grouping together as a unit.

Peter on the roof top seated with the symbolic animals in his lap is great and I feel is in perfect character and harmony with our first Christian martyr Stephen on the other side. I don't see how you can improve that.

If the wine in the Last Supper is changed, likewise the Pentecostal flames and the three border pieces also strengthen the color of the figure to the right of Peter it would be a great improvement. Then I think we would have accomplished all that should be done.

The architects have given you an outstanding Church and it has been so wonderful for one to have been able to create windows as they should have been designed and executed. This has not only been a wonderful experience and opportunity but the result is the greatest triumph. It has all been possible because of the working together and understanding with you and the architect.

What the windows accomplish can be realized when you sit in the sanctuary so you exclude your vision the windows on the Epistle side and vice-versa.

What was also gratifying, while I was there over a dozen people came in for a look and they were all so thrilled.

I wrote this while still in the Sanctuary, but have discussed it with Crosby and Charlie Lawrence, the designer, and they are both in agreement with this report. Charlie has done a consummate job.

Henry Lee Willet-Willet Stained Glass Studios, INC.

Reverend James Thompson to Henry Willet

October 10, 1980

"I was very disappointed that I was not able to be here when you came to review our new windows. I deeply appreciate the report that you recently sent to me. I want you to understand that we are greatly pleased with the windows, and have had a great deal of praise for them from both members and visitors."

"If two small pieces in the "Last Supper" are changed to a burgundy-purple color, and you change the "Pentecostal Flames", the three border pieces and strengthen the color of the figure to the right of Peter in the "Pentecost" arch, then I believe they will be absolutely perfect."

"Thank you for the great joy we have had in working together to create this place of worship."

July 16, 1981

Henry Willet to Reverend Thompson

"I certainly apologize for not reaching you Saturday. Had an early enough appointment to get to Gainesville before noon. I got so involved (In Augusta and Athens) when I pulled my weak mind together, it was too late to phone, which wasn't a bit nice. Sorry. I'll be down again soon and if you are still speaking to me, will be up."

July 21, 1981

Reverend James Thompson to Henry Willet

"I am enclosing a check for $3,000.00 which represents the second 25% payment on one of the small arches in the east elevation of our building."

E. Crosby Willet to Ingrid Barker

January 12, 1982

"I have been meaning to write you for the longest time to thank you for taking me to Gainesville. I was tremendously impressed with the beauty of this building and was glad we had the opportunity to create the glass. Enclosed are some of the better pictures I took that day if you and your dad would like to have any of them."

February 3, 1982

Reverend Thompson to Henry Willet

Dear Henry:

"I am enclosing the down payment for the last of the stained glass windows on the western elevation (New Testament side towards the lake). Work hard and fast, we are anxiously awaiting."

April 20, 1982

Reverend Thompson to Henry Willet

Under separate cover I am sending you the original design with the following suggestions:

1. Keep the locust, do not let it be overpowering.
2. Let the rainbow be a bit more prominent if possible.

June 25, 1982

Reverend James Thompson to Henry Willet

I am enclosing a check for the amount of $5,000.00 as the second 25% payment on the east elevation center panel. I do not recall your having billing us for the second payment on the side panel elevation. I hope this does not mean that you have not started working on that panel. I am very much counting on their being completed and installed by August 1st.

August 9, 1982

Reverend Thompson to Henry Willet on completion of the Old Testament Window

"I love and appreciate you so much that I find it difficult to write this letter, but I am doing so in the knowledge that you would want me to be honest in expressing my feelings about the new window (courtyard side).

"Actually, I'm extremely disappointed with it. It compares so very unfavorable with the existing west window (The New Testament window) that it looks as if it does not belong in the same building with it."

"In general the widow (the Old Testament side) lacks a richness that its west companion has and really looks like a "country cousin" to it."

"I would appreciate it very much if you would come to Gainesville the next time you are down here and view the window yourself. I really do not believe that you will be proud of it."

August 10, 1982

Henry Willet to Reverend James Thompson

"Glad the windows got in. Fine for the wedding. Glad that everybody was happy with them. Will be down before too long and anxious to see the effect in place."

August 13, 1982

Henry Willet to Reverend Thompson

"Dear Jim, I was crushed. I got your letter of August 9, 1982. I'll get down as soon as possible. I do know that Crosby (Henry Willet's son) kept telling to keep this window light- facing the courtyard had much less light than the one looking towards the lake. Sorry."

Cordially,

Henry Willet.

May 10, 1983

Henry Willet to Reverend James Thompson

"I have treated you miserably and no longer worthy to be called a friend."

At Christmas time I got an unwanted present and have just recently gotten off daily radiation treatments and now go back to the hospital on the 23rd of May for an exploratory operation to learn if treatments have been successful."

"Although restricted I have been able to carry on most of the time so I really have no right to use my problem entirely as an excuse and that is why I am ashamed of myself."

We will be installing windows in the First Baptist Church, Augusta in about thirty days and at that time, will plan to come to Gainesville and make those changes. I must get this done because I heard horrible rumors that you were going to pull up stakes in July after all the blood, sweat, tears, struggles with every phase of the work from the architects to worthless stained glass artists in erecting this noble structure to walk off and let someone else enjoy the fruits of your labor ain't too smart."

"I don't expect a robe and ring and a big celebration but if you can find it in your heart to put with me I will be happy. It is horrible when you mess up a beautiful relationship such as we have had."

July 21, 1983

Henry Willet to Reverend James Thompson (Now living in Griffin, Ga.)

"June 1st was one and still is one of the important and happiest days of my life. I had completed my months of daily radiation treatments, and all that went as programed. I had my exploratory operation and received my report and was declared free of the cancer. Now, two months later, four trips back to the hospital, one with pneumonia and still in intense pain and only able to limited getting about with a walker, mostly bedridden. I had been certain condition would have certainly improved long before this and had finally planned to leave for Gainesville Monday when the crew from the studio was going to Georgia to install windows in Augusta, Athens, Savannah, etc. and I was going to come down and work out those changes. Instead I will have to postpone it when I can move about. Sorry to be such a disappointment to you. Hope you are happy in your new work as District Superintendent."

May 17, 1993

Helene Weis (Willet librarian) to John McHugh

"The iconography seems to have been cooperation between Henry Willet and Pastor Thompson. The shape and decorative look were the work of James Barker and his daughter Ingrid. She came for a visit and won all of our hearts, even Henry's, who didn't much like the idea before he met her. At the time she was the only person we knew to have a specialty of ecclesiastical interior decorating."

"The last letter from Henry July 21, 1983 is sad to me. He died quite soon after."

October 1, 1983

Philadelphia Inquirer Obituaries

Henry L. Willet

"Stained glass is a lot more like music than art on a canvas. The vibrations of light coming through the window. The way it reacts to snow on the ground. I don't think any building is complete without God's sunlight coming through the glass and color." Henry Willet 1973

"Henry Lee Willet, 83, the nation's foremost artist in stained glass, died Thursday (September 29) at his home in Wyndmoor. The son of artists who worked in glass, he carried the art to new heights. He made Philadelphia the stained-glass capital of the world."

"He made the Willet Stained Glass Studio, a red-brick plant on East Moreland Avenue of Germantown Avenue in Chestnut Hill, into the largest such facility in the world. The studio has been commissioned to execute more than 10,000 windows over the years."

"Work of the 100 employees at the plant can be seen in public buildings, museums, and churches in every state in the union and in 13 countries abroad."

Joanne Ledwith, (Willet Office Manager) to John McHugh

August, 5 2013

"Now I have spoken to Crosby, regarding his dad. Crosby informed me that Henry had prostate cancer and died from heart issues in combination with the cancer. So now we both know."

Barbara Smith to Crosby Willet

November 14, 1985

"Soon we will be having a dedication service for the beautiful stained glass windows which your company made and installed in our church, and I would greatly appreciate it if you would send us information on the Old Testament and New Testament characters in our windows."

Helene Weis to Ms. Barbara Smith

November 26, 1985

"Here at last is the description of your windows. I contacted Mr. Jim Thompson for help on a few of the scenes that baffled me. I was working from photographs of the original lumiere designs and I realize some changes were made. I believe the subjects did not change. If anything is not as I have described it feel free to change this. It is not sacrosanct. Mr. Thompson and Mr. Henry Willet planned the iconography. Henry has died and Mr. Lawrence the designer does not remember the details. We would like an example of the program or brochure when you have it printed."

The windows in the Sanctuary cost *$98,500.00.*

Willet Stained Glass Studios, Inc.-Philadelphia, Pa. made the windows.

Charles Lawrence designed the iconography.

James E. Barker of Barker and Cunningham- Atlanta, Ga. were the architects.

Where did the stained glass studio leave their mark?

Narthex Entrance/Right panel/Below Francis Asbury (Man on a horse)

November 2014

Jennie Cooper Press

660 A Lanier Park Dr.

Suite A

Gainesville, Ga.

Special thanks to Willet Stained Glass Studios of Philadelphia, Pa., the contributing authors, Billie Thompson, Karen McHugh, Phil DeMore, Dot Dusenberry, Ted and Asden Johnson, Janice Watts, Willis McLemore and Jackie Powers.

Created by

John McHugh

Photography

John McHugh

Illustrations

Taryn Dufault

Karen McHugh

This picture of the old Green Street Church Sanctuary windows was taken by Willis McLemore circa 1965. The only window not currently used in the Thompson Bridge Church is seen at the far right, Girl Pointing to the Ten Commandments.

Made in the USA
Middletown, DE
12 November 2014